MASTERING ME

Keys to living your God-ordained destiny

TONYA HOWARD QUINN

CARLION
PUBLISHERS
SPEAK YOUR BOOK INTO EXISTENCE

Mastering Me: Keys to living your God-ordained destiny
Copyright © 2020 by Tonya Howard Quinn

Editing and typesetting: Inksnatcher.com
Cover design: Camden Lane

Ordering Information: Quantity sales. Special discounts are available on quantity purchases by corporations, associations, and others. For details, contact the author at the email address above.

Mastering Me: Keys to living your God-ordained destiny/Tonya Howard Quinn
ISBN 978-1-7329652-6-3

This book is dedicated to Mike, Justin, Jordan, and Bryson. My family, you have been my place of security, strength, and unconditional love.

CONTENTS

PREFACE

MASTERING AN ACCOMPLISHMENT, technique, or art is to acquire complete knowledge or skill in it. It is also to gain control of or overcome something.

To master something is to obtain a heightened level of knowledge and supernatural ability that puts you over in life. You have a cutting-edge advantage over all things because God is with you. Obstacles don't exist; they are merely opportunities to reveal the heart of God in every situation.

The world's way of doing things is typically based on how *I* can be great, how *I* can make money, how *I* can grow my business. When you center your life on your own personal ability, you are removing the most important element—God. God gives us the power to get wealth and prosperity. Happiness is just a kickback from God because we honor His ways.

God has created a kingdom model that is grounded and rooted in the belief that with Him all things are possible. God's thoughts are far higher than our thoughts, so why not tap into the mind of Christ, especially if you have been doing it your way for years and nothing has come of it.

You're still in the rat race, and you're still unhappy, unmarried, and burdened down with the weights of the world.

The world's way is a clear example of toil: an unrelenting struggle to obtain the things in life others tell you will make you happy. It's not the truth, and I'm here today to bring light to this misconception.

I used to believe mastering something was obtaining the highest level of expertise or competency in an area possible; however, now I realize the concept of *Mastering Me* is a constant evolution. There must be a clear and defined focus on making daily adjustments that leads to a better version of oneself. This can only be done by building a closer relationship with God. Only the creator of a product can reveal the fullness of its purpose. This is why it is so imperative that we begin to ask God questions like:

1. What are you trying to reveal to me about myself that will shift my life for the better?

2. What do you want me to do for your kingdom, God?

3. What is currently in my hands that I can use for your glory?

For the most part, people think they know themselves, but they don't. The enemy has created an illusion in their minds of who they think they are. As a result, most people tend to limit themselves in constant cycles of not feeling good enough, of not deserving certain things in life, and about how far they can go in their own ability.

We tend to only attempt to do things we feel we can accomplish in our own strength. Most people are not even aware the enemy has limited their entire lives and boxed them in, based on *their own* inner critics.

No one has to hold you back from being great if you've mastered that all by yourself. If this is you, this is the day to break the cycle. God wants you to be great and to do great things for His kingdom. Why not start today by being more aware of your thoughts, your words, and your actions? What things are you doing to limit yourself?

I realized one day that my life was in a vicious cycle. I was doing well in my career and making good money, yet I felt terribly unfulfilled. I knew something was missing, and I decided to seek God about it. I told God I would not do one more thing unless I knew His will for my life. I wouldn't make any decisions or major moves; I would do nothing until I heard from God what He had purposed me to do in the earth. In doing that, God began to give me insight and direction on how to realign with the plans of God for my life.

Mastering Me is a book that will enlighten you concerning the importance of pursuing a personal relationship with God and the significance of discovering your purpose. This book will give you a holistic view of strategic self-management God's way.

Have you ever wondered:

- What in the world am I called to do?
- What exactly was I created for?
- What is my purpose?

Sadly enough, these are all questions that many of us struggle with in life. Others never even consider the possibility of purpose because realizing they have lived most of their lives on a train to nowhere is far too devastating to think about. As a result, many never allow themselves the opportunity to consider that there is a place called "Greater."

I had an epiphany one day. God began to enlighten me that I, too, was called for greater things. I had heard of other people being stretched into this "greater" phenomenon—you know, the phenomenon you've read books and heard testimonies about but never had a clue of what that even looked like for you. So sad, but so very true.

In a desperate attempt to keep myself grounded to the monotony of my day, I had allowed patterns and cycles to overtake my life. Distractions, low self-esteem, past experiences, and personal limitations were ruling and reigning in my life. Yes, I allowed them all because they were familiar. Thank God, though, a time comes in life when mediocre is just not good enough. God wants us to be stretched into the full knowledge of who He is and who He has created each and every one of us to be. Most times, the obstacles that hold us back in life are simply what we say about ourselves.

The best person to consult about life mastery is God Himself, the creator of all things. As I began to set my heart to seek God for purpose, God began to give me specific strategies and instructions for dealing with the most difficult obstacle of all—*me!*

Most people will never admit they are the source of their own problems. Sometimes they really don't realize they could be their own worst enemy. God helped me to recognize I was the source of all stagnation in my life. I was the reason why my life seemed to be on a standstill. The reason why I felt unfulfilled was because I lacked a very vital ingredient—the revelation of Christ in me, "Christ in you, the hope of glory" (Colossians 1:27). I was realizing Christ is always at work in me, operating through me, and even pushing through with power on my behalf, *for me!* How could I have ever missed it? My mind, my will, and my emotions were keeping me on a launch pad for decades. *Failure to launch! Failure to launch!* God was flashing this warning light to me loud and clear in hopes that I did not continue to miss it. This time, with clarity of sight—spiritual sight, that is—God began to unlock a wide array of opportunities to shift my entire life for the better.

It was so refreshing to finally understand no one else was standing in my way but *me.* I was the source of all halted momentum in my life because of my own limited thinking. Feelings of unworthiness, not being good enough, and even undeserving of God's best, kept me from years of experiencing the fullness of God in my life.

Once you are able to recognize challenges and interruptions in life as mere distractions, the real work begins. Identify which issues and concerns have taken over your focus, energy, time, and money. Realize that the enemy never wants you to stay focused on the things that bring revelation, insight, wisdom, and the manifestation of all God has intended for you—like prayer, meditating on the Word of God, and making positive confessions. Now take a moment to just pivot. A minor adjustment will yield the best results. Just shift. Shift your focus. Shift your energy. Don't focus on the distraction, focus on God and the distraction will be eliminated. Try it. It really does work. I have receipts!

My prayer is that God will reveal to you who you are in Him as you read further along. I also pray you will know what God's intentions are for your life and that you will never be the same because of it.

God will shift you into the place of purpose to unlock years of unrealized potential in the knowledge of Him.

Limited belief systems prevent many from obtaining any sort of mastery in life. But thank God for Jesus. Today is the day when we can break old patterns, old cycles, and old belief systems.

Tonya Howard Quinn

SPEAK, GOD!

And if you spoke already, what on earth do You sound like?

GROWING UP, THE CLOSEST THING I ever remember to consulting with God on life issues was this book called *Are You There, God? It's Me, Margaret* by Judy Blume. Although I was raised in church for most of my life, I lacked the power of God and felt the absence of the knowledge of Him. I had heard of the God of wrath and the God to be feared, but I was rarely taught of the God of relationship and intimacy. It was in the place of seeking God for who He is, not for what He could give me, that I could uncover my purpose and calling in life.

God wants to give all His children the keys to the kingdom, but with it comes an unraveling of the heart that must be dealt with. In my heart, I knew the answer to finding my purpose was to seek God more intently. As a result, so many questions arose in my head:

1. How do I seek God?
2. How do I delve into hearing the voice of God?
3. How do I have an encounter with God?
4. Is God even talking to me, and if so, how can I discern His voice?
5. Do I need to be at a certain level spiritually to hear from God?

Someone once said to me, "If you can't hear God for yourself, then get around someone who can." This is certainly not meant for you to put all your trust in a man or a woman of God because human nature can be a bit fickle and unpredictable and at times outright contradictory, so only use this as a guide. My pastor often says success leaves clues. If you are lacking in anything, find someone operating in that area at a high level and begin to take notes. You may not be able to use everything from one person, but you can eat the meat and spit out the bones. Only take what is worth repeating and meditating on and leave the rest behind.

No one ever tells you the voice of God occurs in a very familiar way. This is why most people miss it. It comes in the form of a thought—yes, a real thought that pops up in your mind out of nowhere on something you may have absolutely no natural knowledge of. God uses our thoughts as a jumping-off point to begin to unfold information you would not have otherwise known.

God wants us to have the mind of Christ. "For who hath known the mind of the Lord, that he may instruct him? But we have the mind of Christ" (1 Corinthians 2:16). "Let this mind be in you, which was also in Christ Jesus" (Philippians 2:5). "Be not conformed to this world: but be ye transformed by the renewing of your mind, that ye may prove what is that good, and acceptable, and perfect, will of God" (Romans 12:2).

God is a God of relationship. Just like any other valuable relationship, our relationship with Him requires quality time, intimacy, and a thankful heart if we want to usher in the presence of God.

I have heard many people say they have never heard the voice of God or they have never gotten any form of instruction from God. I beg to differ. God is always speaking. Are you quiet enough in your mind and in your spirit to hear Him? The enemy often uses distractions, busyness, and chaos to keep us numb to acknowledging that God really does speak. It's like your friend is trying to call your name when a freight train is coming by at the same time. Odds are you probably won't be able to hear him or her from all the noise, but it doesn't negate the fact that your name was actually being called. You were just unaware it was even happening. Even nonbelievers hear the voice of God. They refer to it as intuition, a gut feeling, or a strong sensing. Yet believers are often the ones with the most contention around hearing God and stepping out on what He is asking them to do.

When I first recognized God was speaking to me, I was driving. I had a vision I was speaking on a platform in front of thousands of people. I was confident, bold, and captivating in my communication with the audience. I knew this vision had to be God because not in a million years would I have desired this for myself. I had a paralyzing fear of public speaking. I had centered my life around avoiding anything and everything that dealt with speaking in public. I even shunned speaking in groups of greater than five people. I know, ridiculous, right? Nevertheless, God had shown me something that was completely beyond anything I could fathom. I just could not get my head around it because it was the total opposite to anything I would have ever hoped for or desired. As a matter of fact, I was offended whenever people would ask me to speak. I would often wonder, *Why in the world do they keep asking me to speak? It's so bizarre.* But what I have learned is that those around you will always point to your place of purpose. Those around you often realize your strengths long before you even get the memo, so pay close attention.

I was unfulfilled. I had a good-paying job in a good career, but my life was not gaining traction, and to me that was a problem. I started to evaluate what was holding me back from getting to this place I knew I was called to, and I sensed limitation preventing me from getting to it. I felt like I was going through a *Groundhog Day* movie, where I'd wake up and follow the exact same routine every day. I started to ask myself real questions like: *What is this? How can I break out of this pattern or the cycle of mediocrity?* On the inside I was living this mediocre life, while on the outside, everybody around my husband and me said we had the best life ever. They saw us as being the role models for both of our families through the things we'd accomplished and things we had; yet on the inside, I felt so unfulfilled. I started praying more to figure out what it was, seeking the Holy Spirit more, asking God questions about what was holding me back.

I began working as a case manager for an insurance company. When I got the job, I was excited. I thought I could do it for the rest of my work life and retire from it—a flexible job with full autonomy and great benefits. One day I woke up and, out of the blue, felt completely different about it. I couldn't breathe thinking about it. I felt that if I stayed in that job one more day, I would literally die.

At that time, I was not close with God. I went to church but had not received the Holy Spirit and the gift of speaking in tongues. I understood the concept of God but not the Holy Spirit. Yet that's when the thought hit me to go back to school.

I've never been a person to want to return to school or to seek a title. When people asked if I would go back to school, I would say, No way, never *ever*. But it hit me like a ton of bricks to go back and get my degree. I thought, *Why in the world do I need to do that?* but I felt strongly in my spirit that it was God nudging me, telling me it was time to go back to school. I decided to attempt to get my nurse practitioner degree.

I wound up going back to school in my forties. It was a lot of hard work, but it was not as difficult as I'd thought it would be. In high school I did the bare minimum to get by. We could get on the honor roll with Cs, so my friends and I did not strive beyond that—that was mediocre living, which trickled down into my everyday life. But then, in my forties I made a decision to change and do more than basic. I challenged myself. I focused. I wanted to get both my bachelor's and master's degrees. Anything below an A was unacceptable. I wound up getting both degrees with a 4.0 GPA. I began to realize I could have pushed myself through high school in the same way. It was all in my attitude and in my level of focus and determination.

Mastering Me

— 2 —

MASTERING ME

No more fighting

I WAS BORN IN A LITTLE TOWN called Natchez in Mississippi. My mother got pregnant with me at the age of fourteen and gave birth to me at fifteen. Due to the closeness in age, my mother and I were raised almost as sisters because my grandmother raised me almost like a daughter. She had four other kids, who all directed me and had an authoritative role in my life on what I could or couldn't do. Growing up, I felt I had multiple sets of parents telling me what to do. It made me feel extremely displaced.

One person would give me permission, and then another would veto it. I ended up having to go through two or three people to get approval to do anything. "Can I go to the game tonight?" My mom would say, "Yes, you can," but then my grandmother would come back with, "I had a dream last night, and I don't feel good about it; I feel something's going to happen. Don't go to that game." My mom would say, "You can go and hang out with this group," but then my grandmother would say, "I heard negative things about that family. I don't think you need to hang around them." I could never plan my life based on just one person's approval. Going through many different people to get approval to do anything was crazy.

My grandmother was prophetic, although she did not know it. She would sense things before they happened. My grandfather was a pastor. I grew up in the church but never understood the Holy Spirit because we were raised Baptist. Baptists tend to take the Holy Spirit out of the equation. My grandparents used to say things like, "Those people speak in tongues over there; don't go to that church." We thought speaking in tongues was only meant for the Bible days. We never even considered the idea that speaking in tongues was a powerful gift and the major thing we needed. We stayed away from all of that. Since my grandfather was a pastor, we were at the church from sunup to sundown, and we traveled to his different speaking engagements and local revivals. Like I said, we were in the church house all the time.

Yet still I knew things. I considered myself wise because people often came to me for advice. I would give them my thoughts, which I understand now was God speaking to me and directing my steps. On one occasion I was hanging out with friends in the parking lot. We were standing around and talking when suddenly I felt it was time to leave. *Let's go now!* I later learned that after I left, someone came and killed the guy I had been talking to just moments before. God always kept me covered when I listened to my instincts, but I didn't realize it was God leading me all along.

MASTERING MARRIAGE

My husband and I got married at a very young age. I was nineteen years old and he was twenty-one. We had a quick courtship and decided to get married within a year of dating. Most people thought I was pregnant when we got married because we were getting married so quickly. But *no!* I was not pregnant! It took us six years before I got pregnant with the twins. People are something else.

Early on in our marriage, I really struggled. I was an alpha female married to a class A alpha male. He was a workaholic trying to provide for his family and move up the corporate ladder. At nineteen years of age, I had no idea what that meant. All I knew was he was rarely at home and he was always working. In my mind, this equated that I was not a priority. I totally couldn't see his point of view on this. All I knew was he was never home.

So I thought since he was never home, I'd go home every weekend, which was a two-hour drive one way. I did this for a few weekends, until one day my husband told me, "Look, you can't be going home every weekend to see your family. I'm your family now." I thought to myself, *He must be out of his mind. How is he gonna tell me I can't go home when he's never here anyway?* My grandma told me he was right, but I did not want to relinquish my control. It was one of the toughest things I ever had to do. I cried for a couple of weeks because I was in a new town and I knew no one there. My husband had a conversation with me about it and said it was an opportunity to meet new people. Of course, because I'm an introvert, there was no way I was buying that excuse. Then finally I caved and accepted I had to make the best of it. And I did. I began to meet new people. I came out of my shell more. I was able to interact with strangers without feeling out of place. The whole experience really grew me as a person. Who knew?

Imagine the things you'll discover about yourself when you allow yourself to experience uncomfortable situations. I now believe it's in the place of uncomfortableness that we grow exponentially into our best selves.

I remember another situation that caused a lot of contention in our marriage. We had got into an argument, and we were scheduled to go to his mom's house for a family function. Of course, since I was blazing-hot mad, I told him there was no way I was going with him to his mom's house, he could forget it. So he went without me. He later told me everyone kept asking about me the whole night and that it just didn't feel right with me not being there. Then he said, "So going forward, we are going to be together no matter what. If you are mad or not, we stick together." I thought, *This guy is nuts! I'm not doing that!* But he was so persistent, I gave in and went along with the plan. I can honestly say that was the best decision we ever made for our marriage. Oftentimes we would make up while we were there, and no one ever knew we were upset with one another. The other thing we agreed on was that we would keep personal details of our marriage between the two of us, which was true wisdom at its best.

Our kids tell their friends we never argue, and of course their friends think they are not telling the truth, but it's true we never argue anymore. We may have occasional disagreements, but we never raise our voices to one another, and we always apologize as soon as possible to ensure there is no bitterness between us, ever. There is real power in growing in wisdom.

Our marriage has not been perfect by any means, but it has been fruitful. We have grown into better versions of ourselves. My husband has evolved into having a balanced lifestyle—God first then family being his top priorities. Although our business is important to us, it takes a back seat to family any day of the week.

I have been married now for almost twenty-eight years. We had to learn how to make our marriage work through trial and error. Here are some helpful keys to having a successful marriage:

1. BE QUICK TO FORGIVE. You can expect challenges and obstacles along the way in any marriage; however, it's how you deal with those challenges that makes you an overcomer or a victim. Keeping God first and in the center of things is the best advice I could ever give you. Pray together as often as you can. God will protect and preserve your marriage. Don't hold on to past hurts. Let them go. The more you hold on to, the more paranoid, suspicious, and distrustful you will become. No marriage can withstand distrust. Trust is the foundation on which marriages must stand, and if there is no trust, your marriage is doomed from the start.

2. ALWAYS CONSIDER THE OTHER PERSON'S POINT OF VIEW. There are always two different perspectives in a marriage. There will always be a time when someone will need to bend. I heard someone say once, "That which is flexible will never break." Flexibility is essential in marriage. You should always use wisdom in discerning which situations to bend on. I always try to see things from my husband's point of view and vice versa. Sometimes we have to agree to disagree and let the chips fall where they may, but usually those experiences become life lessons for us.

3. PICK YOUR BATTLES. Sometimes you will have to plead your case and stand firm on occasional family issues, but if these types of situations occur too frequently, realize this is a danger zone that can cause tremendous rifts in your marriage. The best way to make this as peaceful as possible is to communicate, communicate, communicate. Lack of communication or miscommunication, in my opinion, is one of the number one causes of divorce.

4. STAY CLOSE. STAY BALANCED. DON'T ALLOW YOUR LIVES TO REVOLVE AROUND YOUR CHILDREN. I'm not saying you shouldn't value your children and ensure their needs are met; however, we put our marriage first and the kids second. Most people who put their children before their spouses typically wind up getting divorced when the kids leave home. This is truly no way to live.

I'm not saying you shouldn't protect your kids. I'm saying the best way to ensure a healthy environment for your children is to model a healthy relationship between the parents. If you stay in an unhealthy marriage for the kids, realize you are modeling total relationship dysfunction. Your kids will pick this up, and they will carry the torch you give them. More often than not, children model what they see more than what you say. If you're staying, get healing and learn how to display healthy relationship skills.

5. NEVER STOP DATING. Schedule one-on-one time with one another as often as possible. We try to do date night at least twice a month. Now that the kids are growing up,

17

we have more opportunities to schedule time together. *When you like your husband, you will always find ways to hang out with him, no matter what.* Notice I said *like.* You can love your husband and totally dislike him. Don't you have family members you love but don't like so much? Be honest. I know I do. I absolutely like my husband a whole lot, and I prefer him over anyone else in the world. He's my BFF.

6. PUT EACH OTHER FIRST. I always put my husband before anyone else. *Of course* he comes before any friend or family member. I put him first, but I still maintain other relationships. My friendships are still intact. We just put our needs as a couple above every other relationship.

7. NEVER TAKE OUTSIDE ADVICE ABOUT MAJOR DECISIONS IN YOUR MARRIAGE. KEEP YOUR FRIENDS AND FAMILY OUT OF YOUR MARRIAGE. It's important to ensure that any decisions you make in your marriage are your own. Everyone has an opinion, so never allow others to force their opinions on what's best for your marriage. I'm not saying don't listen to good counsel or good wisdom. What

if your spouse did something that created a wedge in the relationship? You go tell your friend about it, and now she's telling you you should leave and get a divorce and all this. The crazy thing is, it's oftentimes the friend who doesn't even have a husband. Or it's the friend whose own marriage is a complete wreck. Bottom line is, always consider the fruit of the ones you take counsel from. If you are going to make a major life decision about your marriage, make sure it's based on what you want, not the opinions of just anyone.

MASTERING MIRACLES

I call this chapter "Mastering Miracles," but honestly, I am still learning about the supernatural. Even still, some miraculous things have occurred that prove God's *dunamis* power.

We'd gone on a cruise to the Bahamas, and my youngest son came back as a souvenir, if you get my drift. I was not trying to get pregnant.

I was having my own internal struggles concerning this pregnancy. We were living in Atlanta. I already had two-year-old twins still in diapers. I was away from my family and did not have any close relatives nearby. I was feeling overwhelmed, and my husband was a workaholic because he was trying to provide for us.

My two little ones needed my attention. My stress level was extremely high. One of the twins was colicky and cried all the time. I had little peace, and the thought of another child was overwhelming. *I'm definitely not ready for another one.* I was dealing with postpartum depression with the twins too, although I didn't know it.

When you're suffering from postpartum depression, your mind does not process information properly; you can do and say things that are not part of your normal personality. This was what was happening to me.

We were referred to a specialist who found tumors in my baby's head—an extremely serious condition. The tumors started small. First there were two, and then every time we went to the doctor, the number of tumors increased. There were so many, they couldn't count them. They kept saying this child would be born severely mentally retarded and that I needed to decide if I was going to have an abortion because he would be physically unable to care for himself.

I began to pray for a miracle—for my baby to get healed. Then we started praying as a family, which I fondly called our prayer line. We corporately prayed as a family that the tumors would disappear. Weeks later, God miraculously healed him. Even the doctor said it was a miracle.

We ended up delivering this perfect baby. When we took him back to the doctor, he said, "This is a miracle because there are no more tumors." Bryson was born healthy and weighed nine pounds. At first he didn't pass his hearing test, and I thought, *Maybe it's the residual effects of his tumors,* but no. He is such an articulate child, wise beyond his years.

The enemy tried to snatch Bryson from my life before he could enter the world, but I serve a God of miracles.

MASTERING HOW I SHOW UP IN THE WORLD

I had an internal battle going on. I later realized I was fighting two ways of thinking. On the inside, I had a different narrative going on about myself than the narrative in the minds of those around me. Their positive perspective was contradicting the negative story I was telling myself. When I realized this, I started to make the change in my thinking. I wanted to be different. I wanted to be able to communicate with people effectively.

I often felt misunderstood. Whenever I expressed my opinion, my husband would always say, "No, think about it this way," because he was wise beyond his years, even in his twenties. He's a brilliant man, and he would always say, "What if they meant it this way?" He would always give me an alternate perspective to the way I was viewing things, which was usually skewed. That's when I realized my thought process was based on my past experiences and not the truth. It wasn't even reality; it was my made-up, alternate reality I had created on the inside. It was my own personal story that was not true to what was going on around me; it was false. It was FEAR manifesting—False Evidence Appearing Real.

I had to confront the fact that I was angry at almost everything. I was angry at my upbringing, being raised by a fourteen-year-old mother. I secretly resented her because she could never give me what I needed. It took me years to understand she was only a teenager when she had me, just a child having a child. Before she had me, she had dreams about going to college, but all that was taken away from her because she had a baby at such a young age. I became the focal point of everything that had been taken away in her life, the source of why all of her dreams would never come true. She told me stories about people shunning her when she got pregnant. Everybody pulled away from her, including close family members. As a result, I was raised in a household with a mother who never showed love. She was cold, verbally and physically abusive, introverted, and outright mean. Of course I was angry.

My mother developed a coping mechanism to keep herself in a shell so she wouldn't get hurt. Doing that meant everybody outside that shell had to be pushed far away. She would often push me and my sister away from her. We never had a close relationship with my mom because of that. She internalized her anger, and I reproduced the same type of behavior in my life.

As a child, my mom would lock herself up in her room for days and not come out. As an adult, I did this to my family. My mom had major depression. Many women suffer from this debilitating disease all over the world, yet few admit it is a real problem that requires treatment. It's paralyzing at times. I had internalized that too, but my relationship with my husband changed all of that. I would tell my kids and husband, "Don't disturb me, don't come in here. I'm staying in this room. I don't want to see or talk to anyone." I did this for a while, but then one day my husband said, "Look. We're not going to do that. I don't know what's going on with you or how you were raised, but it is not normal for you to lock up in a room away from your family for days at a time." For me it was normal because that's what I saw my mom do.

It was a good thing for him to put his foot down and say "No, you're not doing that." He snatched me out of the worst form of self-abuse I could do to myself. And it *is* self-abuse and self-hatred because you isolate yourself to the point where you feel all alone, even when you have people around you who love you and want to have you with them. He snatched me out of that behavior, and that stopped me from being a self-imposed introvert.

I was an undercover introvert, yet I would talk to everybody. I had friends, but I preferred to be by myself. Everybody thought I was extroverted, but I had this other internal battle going on. I was able to stop the generational curse of depression most of the women in my family dealt with because my husband showed me a better way.

I was open to trying to become a better version of myself, and this is what totally began to shift my entire life. I was in pursuit of happiness—real happiness. You know, the kind of happiness that makes you smile for no apparent reason other than just being alive.

Oftentimes, God sends disrupters into our lives to disrupt lifelong patterns and cycles that keep us trapped in these antiquated states of being. The disrupters are really gifts from God, if you recognize the Sender. My husband was my disrupter, and he challenged me on so many things, which has resulted in a revolutionary change in all areas of my life for the better.

I challenge you to begin to recognize the disrupters in your life. They may come in the form of a friend who challenges you on the things you say or do, or even a child who calls you out on your

ways, or maybe even a coworker. God will send disrupters to show up any way He chooses. The main
thing to remember is to not miss the disrupters,
however they may show up. It's God sending you
an opportunity to perfect some things in your life,
all for your good.

Most of us are unaware of how we show up in
the world. We are so used to being the way we are
that we never examine ourselves. The Word of God
says "Let us test and examine our ways and let us
return to the Lord" (Lamentations 3:40 AMPC).
We should be constantly evaluating ourselves to
see if there is anything we could have said or done
better for the glory of God. Don't assume people
knowing who you are and how you act gives you a
pass to be mean or hurtful to others. God is watching, and you're going to have to give an account of
every word and every action.

Be quick to forgive and quick to apologize. Bitterness, resentfulness, unforgiveness, shame, and
condemnation are some of the enemy's clever
tricks to keep you bound and limited in life. If you
begin to release even the hidden things—the
things you are most ashamed of—then the enemy

can no longer torment you about them. There is freedom in releasing hidden things.

If you survived trauma, chances are you can help someone else survive what would have killed most people. That alone is a story of triumph. I encourage you to share your story. Anything you keep hidden becomes a tool for the enemy to torment you with. There is power and liberation in sharing your testimony. "Who the son sets free is free indeed" (John 8:36). Starting today, allow your life to be a testimony, not a trap or a tool to be used by the enemy however he chooses. Take back your freedom today.

It really does matter how you show up in the world. People are watching you, and they are learning and taking notes from everything you do. I would much rather they pick up positive influences from me rather than negative ones. I choose to be a positive change agent.

- 3 -

THE HOLY SPIRIT

Given to us

AFTER HIS RESURRECTION, Jesus's disciples asked Him to stay, and He said, "The Comforter has to come back because He's going to tell you things. He's going to be able to do things for you that I couldn't do in this fleshly body" (John 14:26, paraphrased). That Scripture sets the precedence of how important the Holy Spirit is because if the Holy Spirit guides you into all truth, you don't need to worry about what to do next. Many try to do things in their own ability and get fearful because of the unknown. All of your fear can be eradicated by simply knowing you can trust the Holy Spirit, who is life's ultimate tour guide. Even when the fear is there, you can have a relentless trust in God that is so solid that you move forward in spite of fear, knowing God has your back through it all. That's the foundation of faith—real faith, tried and true.

The Holy Spirit shifts the way you think about things. He shifts your perspective and your views and begins to realign your will with the will of God for your life. The Holy Spirit is light years ahead of achieving what you could have done in your own strength.

The Holy Spirit has already been given to us. A lot of people think they have to tarry for the Holy Spirit or that He only comes to some people. That's a misconception. The Holy Spirit is not limited to a few people; He's a free gift for all believers. Know He's available to you, and if you decide today, in this moment, that you want the Holy Spirit, He can come into your life and you can have Him with you at all times.

Do you want to receive the Holy Spirit?

"Then Peter said unto them, Repent, and be baptized every one of you in the name of Jesus Christ for the remission of sins, and ye shall receive the gift of the Holy Ghost." (Acts 2:38)

"When Paul had laid [his] hands upon them, the Holy Ghost came on them; and they spake with tongues, and prophesied." (Acts 19:6)

Having the Holy Spirit in your life shifts you to where you are always "in the know" about what's happening. You don't even have to worry about what's going to occur because even when you don't know what's going on, God does.

I woke up one morning and heard myself saying, "Even when I don't know, I still know. I know what's going on, even when I don't know." I said this all day long. The Lord led me to a Scripture in John, "Whatever [the Holy Spirit] hears He will speak; and He will tell you things to come" (John 16:13). This Scripture is precisely the reason you don't have to be paranoid about being connected to the wrong people because God will always reveal the hidden things. God is the one who protects us always through it all because of His grace.

Isolating yourself from establishing healthy relationships is a trick of the enemy to keep you secluded and lonely. The enemy uses seclusion and isolation to trap you in a place where he can have full access to your thoughts, your will, and your emotions. This is a very dangerous place to be.

"If either of them falls down, one can help the other up. But pity anyone who falls and has no one to help them up" (Ecclesiastes 4:10 NIV). "For where two or three gather in my name, there am I with them" (Matthew 18:20 NIV). This shows the power of unity. Going through life thinking you can make it on your own is a lie from the pit of hell. We need one another. We need good healthy relationships. We need friends who will encourage us, motivate us, push us to do greater, give us wise counsel, comfort us, edify us, and exhort us. It's all part of God's plan. Trust God and He will reveal the intentions of the people you choose to associate with. Surrender it all to God and watch your life shift completely to producing the kind of relationships you've always imagined.

MY FIRST ENCOUNTER WITH THE HOLY SPIRIT

I have encountered God's Holy Spirit for many years, even as a young girl. I never realized it because I just wasn't taught about it. Just like I said earlier, I remember a time when I was driving and

I had a vision of myself speaking to large crowds, which filled me with dread. Of course I asked God why in the world would He ask me to do that, but He never answered because He had shown me His desire in the vision.

HOW TO RECEIVE THE HOLY SPIRIT

> But the Helper (Comforter, Advocate, Intercessor—Counselor, Strengthener, Standby), the Holy Spirit, whom the Father will send in My name [in My place, to represent Me and act on My behalf], He will teach you all things. And He will help you remember everything that I have told you.
>
> – John 14:26 AMP

> When the day of Pentecost had come, they were all together in one place, and suddenly a sound came from heaven like a rushing violent wind, and it filled the whole house where they were sitting. There appeared to them tongues resembling fire, which were being distributed [among them], and they rested on each one of them [as each person received the Holy Spirit]. And they were all filled [that is, diffused throughout their being] with the Holy Spirit and began to speak in other tongues (different languages), as the Spirit was giving them the ability to speak out [clearly and appropriately].
>
> – Acts 2:1-4 AMP

The single most important thing that can happen to you as a believer is receiving the Holy Spirit. The most important thing is to have the desire in your heart to receive Holy Spirit and then set yourself apart and pray, asking God to fill you with His precious Holy Spirit.

The evidence you are filled with the Holy Spirit is that you will speak in tongues—God's way of having a secure line with you no one else can listen in on—and God will give you heaven's agenda for your life and provide the step-by-step instructions on how to walk it out. "Anyone who speaks in a tongue does not speak to people but to God. Indeed, no one understands them; they utter mysteries by the Spirit" (1 Corinthians 14:2 NIV)

Who wouldn't want this? It's like having an advantage over everyone else because of who you are in relationship with—our heavenly Father. This is God's desire—for us all to have this advantage in every area of our lives so we can have sweat-less victories. There is no toil with this, only countless breakthroughs in every situation. This is not just for me; everyone in God's kingdom was created for greatness.

As I said before, I was raised a Baptist, and Baptists tend to have a red flag on the Holy Spirit, but something in me knew I needed to be filled and baptized in the Holy Spirit with the evidence of speaking in tongues. I had no idea how to get there though. I had been prayed for to receive tongues but had never really experienced it, so I pressed my way in.

I remember saying over and over, "I receive your Holy Spirit with the evidence of speaking in tongues." Then I would hear myself babbling, so I would say it under my breath because my mind wouldn't allow me to believe it was God. I had all sorts of thoughts: *This is crazy. You are worshiping the devil! This is not tongues; you don't sound like anyone else who speaks in tongues.*

This was the enemy not wanting me to take ownership of what was given to us long ago. Jesus said, "But you shall receive power when the Holy Spirit comes on you" (Acts 1:8 NIV). What I failed to understand was that the Holy Spirit was a gift given to me by Christ, and I had access to it; all I had to do was receive and take it by faith. So I slowly but surely increased the volume of my tongues until I was full out speaking with

35

authority. Then I began teaching everyone else I knew about the importance of receiving tongues: my mom, other family members, and just regular people, until they all began to speak in tongues.

— 4 —

DISCERNING THE VOICE OF GOD

Through your mind

THE MIND NEEDS TO BE RENEWED DAILY in order to discern the voice of God. When your mind is renewed, you have achieved 90 percent of the task of discerning the voice of God.

> And do not be conformed to this world [any longer with its superficial values and customs], but be transformed and progressively changed

[as you mature spiritually] by the renewing of your mind [focusing on godly values and ethical attitudes], so that you may prove [for yourselves] what the will of God is, that which is good and acceptable and perfect [in His plan and purpose for you].

-Romans 12:2 AMP

Before you became a Christian, your mind was trained to believe the world's system and its norms. And the belief of the world is contrary to the belief of God. When you give your life to Christ, your spirit is born again but not your mind. In order to begin discerning the voice of God, it is necessary that your mind be renewed. This is because one major way to discern the voice of God is through your mind, which is your thought-processing channel.

God's voice comes across to me as a thought. It's very similar to my own thoughts. This is why most people miss God's communication methods. The Word of God says we have "the mind of Christ" (1 Corinthians 2:16), so if that is true, we can begin to get God's thoughts, His ideas, His belief system, and His creative ability. Scripture also references the voice of God as a "still small voice" (1 Kings 19:9–12). Most people are waiting for this huge, life-altering encounter with God. That is a possibility, but they miss God in His silence, in His whisper, in His presence, if that's all they're looking for.

God also speaks through His Word, the Bible. As I read the Bible, as I'm led by the Holy Spirit to read and search out and study the Word, revelation is poured out to me that leads to specific instructions. I know my God, and I will never follow the voice of a stranger (see John 10:4–5).

Your life is centered around the direction God leads you in. It is important to discern the voice of God because His voice is the original navigation system for your life. For this to happen, you need the Holy Spirit.

I never understood fully what intimacy with God truly meant, so my intimacy was through my Baptist pastor. I thought if I needed to hear from God or get a prayer to God, all I needed to do was just talk to the pastor, and he would mediate for me. Needless to say, my family and I weighed down the pastor with a lot of our issues and requests.

Just to be clear, there will be times when you ask for prayer from others, but that should never replace your personal relationship with God. We should always be in constant, direct prayer with

God for ourselves. It is not a task you should just give over to someone else in hopes that she or he will give God the message for you. God wants each and every one of us to be able to come boldly to the throne of grace on our own behalf (Hebrews 4:16). I typically never read the Bible except when I was at church, and that was the extent of my relationship with God = absolutely no relationship.

THE CALL OF GOD

When I was younger, I always heard my name being called in my mind, but I was advised never to answer. I was told it was the devil calling me. But as I began to read the Bible on my own, I read the story of Eli and Samuel. I saw how Eli taught Samuel to answer to the voice of God.

> (Now Samuel did not yet know the LORD, nor was the word of the LORD yet revealed to him.) And the LORD called Samuel again the third time. So he arose and went to Eli, and said, "Here I am, for you did call me."
> Then Eli perceived that the LORD had called the boy. Therefore Eli said to Samuel, "Go, lie down; and it shall be, if He calls you, that you must say, 'Speak, LORD, for Your servant hears.'" So Samuel went and lay down in his place.

Now the LORD came and stood and called as at
other times, "Samuel! Samuel!"
And Samuel answered, "Speak, for Your servant hears."
Then the LORD said to Samuel: "Behold, I will
do something in Israel at which both ears of
everyone who hears it will tingle."

- 1 Samuel 3:7-11 NKJV

This Scripture settled my confusion on who was
calling me in my spirit. I decided to develop a
deeper relationship with God, and each time in my
devotion time I would say, "Speak, Lord, Your
servant is listening." Then I would wait after I said
that to see what I would hear.

Then I would hear, "Get your pen," and He
would begin to give me downloads. I wrote "Communion with God" as my journal title, and then
later I started titling it "God Speaks." I would
journal everything. First He told me about who I
was, and then He began to shift my perspective on
what I thought about myself. He began to validate
who I was on the inside as well as who He created
me to be. That shifted my whole perspective because I went from *Is this you, God? Did you say
that? Is this coming from my head? Surely, I didn't
hear that! Am I thinking this all by myself?* to
thinking, *It's got to be God because I would never*

think about myself like this. That's when I started to discern what was my voice, what was God's voice, and what was the enemy's voice.

I based this off the knowledge that whatever God tells you, Scripture is always going to validate it; and whenever He gave me a word I felt strongly in my heart about, I would say, "God, I know this, I feel this in my spirit, but where is this coming from? Show me this in your Word." And He would point my eyes on the Scripture that proved it was true. It's amazing. Oftentimes when I do that, He takes me right to the Word. That's how I started the discernment process. Anytime God speaks to me, He validates it with Scripture.

Once my thinking was changed about my identity, I began to pray for a deeper understanding and knowledge of God and who He has created me to be. A whole new experience has awakened in me. I now hear the voice of God and understand His instruction. He now speaks to me directly, and I no longer need a mediator to reach Him. I speak prophetically to teach others, which has opened them up to desiring more of God as well. I now can feel God's presence, and I know for sure He is always with me in every area of my life. I no longer have to do things in my own strength because my God is with me.

Nothing else in this world is quite like it—having a heavenly Father who loves you despite everything you've done—good, bad, or ugly. God is a forgiving God, and understanding His love for us is revolutionary. A game changer for sure.

HOW TO DISCERN HIS VOICE

- Be born again.

- Desire to receive the baptism of the Holy Spirit.

- Pray. Start by asking questions about your life. Ask God about every aspect of your life.

- Put your challenges into perspective and study what the Scriptures say concerning personal challenges. Then align your mind to the will and the Word of God concerning any given situation or challenge. If you have challenges with money, find out from Scripture what it says about finances. If you have a problem with fear, find out what the Scriptures say about fear.

- Read the Word regularly and find a translation that makes it easy for you to understand. Some of my favorite translations include the Amplified Bible (AMP), New King James Version (NKJV), New International Version (NIV), English Standard Version (ESV), The Passion Translation (TPT), and The Message (MSG). In all my years, I had never had a tangible desire to read the Word of God, but I was now being drawn to study. I was thinking I needed more training on *how* to study the Bible, but the Holy Spirit is the best teacher. Daily meditation of God's Word brings revelation. The more and more you study the Word of God, the more God will unlock mysteries and give you clear insight so you can know and understand God's truth. "But whenever anyone turns to the Lord, the veil is taken away" (2 Corinthians 3:16 NIV). This means the truth that was once hidden is now revealed because God wants you to win.

- Meditate on the promises of God. Much of the time we allow certain things to exist in our lives because we think they're normal,

not knowing God has dealt with every obstacle for us through Jesus. It is only when
you read and meditate on the Scriptures
that the Holy Spirit reveals some of these
truths to you.

Nothing is more important in life than setting
your heart to obtain a level of mastery in hearing
the voice of God. I believe that the more and more
you grow in God, the more He will continue to ex-
pound on the ways He communicates with you.
There is no formula for communicating and devel-
oping a relationship with God. You think you just
have to pray twenty minutes in tongues, then read
the Word for ten minutes a day, and you've got it?
No! God is always mixing things up as He so
chooses so that when you hear God's voice and recognize it, you can pray for as long as He wants you
to. God may unction you to effortlessly extend
your prayer time because you have a burden to intercede for someone. Prayer is not all about us,
what we want, what our family wants or needs, or
what I need for my business; this is about how we
can be used by God to reveal His glory on the earth.

MASTERING CLARITY

I miss it sometimes. Everybody misses it. Nobody's perfect. I admit to missing it. I don't always take heed of the Word. One day the Lord told me "Now is the time when you need to declutter and get organized because if you don't do it early, you're going to be overwhelmed toward the end of the year." Now I'm working on a book, and I'm trying to open a clinic. God warned me. I missed it. I didn't do it. But that's why failure is so important—next time I will be sure to pay more attention and do what He says. I missed it that time, but I'm not going to freak out about it. I am going to master today what I missed yesterday. I know next time when He tells me to do something, I should go ahead and do it because obedience is imperative in my walk with God.

And with God, there is absolutely no toil; that's why He says, "My yoke is easy and my burden is light" (Matthew 11:28–30). Whatever He tells you to do although it may seem difficult at the time, with God, it becomes easy. You have to know that whenever you're toiling for something, it doesn't mean you don't have to work hard for it. If you're lazy, you're going to think you can just sit back and everything's going to come to you. No, it doesn't work like that. You still must do the work, but in doing the work, it's an easy thing. It's an easy production—everything comes effortlessly because He's giving you the downloads of everything you need in every moment outside your capability.

One time I prophesied to one of my life group members that God was going to start sending her people to buy products from her. She had made a beautiful journal for young girls. One day she got a call from a guy asking if she had any journals for young girls, but she told him she didn't. He needed writing prompts for the young girls, and she didn't have the writing prompts in hers, so she referred him to someone else until she got hers ready. In that moment God gave me a word for her. I said, "You call him back. You tell him you'll have it in less than two weeks because the moment you sit down, God's going to give you a supernatural download. You're going to create this journal. You're going to sell it, and not only are you going to sell it, but you're going to produce it for schools. Schools will align with the style of this journal, and other people will begin to call you about it. It's going to be difficult in your own strength, but God is going to produce it effortlessly through you, and it won't feel like toil."

Here is her boundary, here's the mental block: *Because I don't have it perfect, because I don't have step-by-step instructions on how to do it, then I'm going to say no.* How often do we all do this? God begins saying things to us, and we look at it based on our ability and think we can't get it done, so we automatically say no. But God wanted her to see things from His perspective. God told me to tell her, "He says He's not looking for your perfection, He's looking for your purity of heart. He's looking for your heart because what's in you is enough." She broke down and started crying. I checked on her the next day, and she said she'd stayed up until one o'clock doing the prompts. God supernaturally gave her what she needed for the journal.

It blows my mind when people share their stories. That is why testimony is important: the power of testimony is valuable.

— 5 —

WATCH IN PRAYER

See heaven intervene

FOR ALL CHILDREN OF GOD, prayer should be one of the most essential aspects of our lives. The Word says to "pray without ceasing" (1 Thessalonians 5:17).

Prayer is one of the major ways we humans can effectively communicate with God. We can only do that through prayer, which is the conduit by which the supernatural intervenes in response to the natural.

> Praying at all times in the Spirit, with all prayer
> and supplication. To that end keep alert with
> all perseverance, making supplication for all
> the saints.
>
> — Ephesians 6:18 ESV

Prayer is very vital. At first I thought that people who pray all the time had something wrong with them. *Who does that? That's unrealistic.* Now I see what they were doing by praying. When you are in relationship with God, communication is always going on between you and Him. It's like when something is happening in your life, you want to call your friend or your spouse and talk about it. That's the way my relationship with God is in the place of prayer. Whenever something happens, I ask, "God, what do you think about this? What are you trying to say? What are you trying to show me about this?" I include Him in every aspect of my life through prayer.

Prayer averts the plans and plots of the enemy. It's often necessary that we don't see what's coming around the bend, but you know that when your spirit is ushered into prayer, a lot of people call it a "burden." I call it a "weight" to pray; when I get weights to pray about different people, then I go ahead and pray because I know God is trying to get me somewhere in the Spirit with that prayer. He's trying to do something on their behalf with that prayer.

When you are in constant fellowship with the Holy Spirit, He can help you avoid a lot of problems you wouldn't ordinarily know how to avoid. For example, I was walking through my neighborhood one day and praying. I had just talked to my husband—he was on the plane about to fly home— and the Holy Spirit urged me to pray in the Spirit immediately in that moment. I prayed in tongues for about fifteen minutes, when my husband called me back and said, "Hello, babe, I'm not going to be home in time because the plane I was scheduled to be on is having mechanical issues, so they're sending us in another plane." I believed that prayer I prayed at that moment averted whatever evil plan the enemy had against my husband's journey.

IMPORTANCE OF PRAYER

The importance of prayer can never be overemphasized. I was praying in tongues one day, and I started travailing in the Spirit. This had never happened to me before. I didn't know what I was praying, but I knew I was travailing in the Spirit. I started asking God, "Who is this person I'm

51

praying for?" because the Bible encourages us to ask for interpretation of our tongues (see 1 Corinthians 14:13). The moment I asked, I saw a vision of my mom. I kept praying in tongues, weeping in the Spirit. After a couple of hours, I got a release in my spirit. When I stopped praying, the Lord instructed me saying, "Call your mom. Tell her you're coming, go to her house, anoint the place, and take her out to eat. Tell her you just came down to spend some time with her." I did as I was told. I spent the day with her. That night, as I started praying, the Holy Spirit said, "Lay hands on your mom's stomach." As I did that, she passed out under the anointing on the couch. I kept praying in the Spirit. The Lord opened my spiritual eyes and I saw a hand around her neck, so I asked her, "Are you having tension around your neck?" She said, "Yes, it's been bothering me all week. It feels like a hand is around my neck." I commanded the tension to leave, and it released her immediately.

I told her I wanted to anoint the house. She said, "I've been praying for the pastor to come over and anoint my house, and look! The Lord sent my child down here to anoint my house." Isn't God amazing? He will reveal the hidden things to you so the needs of those you love will be attended to.

Through that experience, God saved my mom from whatever evil plan the enemy had against her, and He rectified and mended some broken places in our relationship too. It was so God from the beginning to the end. My mom has truly been growing more in God every day. She once told me, "I want to be like you when I grow up." Truly, it was one of the best compliments I could have ever received from my mom. God has truly revived my mom's life, and she is evolving into the person God intended her be every day. I thank God for her transformation. It has truly been a blessing.

TRAVAILING IN THE SPIRIT

Travailing is a deep-seated cry to God in a place of prayer. You're crying out to Him in a deep way for His power or for Him to intercede in a certain area. You are crying out in the Spirit for the mercy and power of God to intervene. When you are travailing, you're not thinking about anything, you're just left alone with God in the deep place. Travailing, to my knowledge, is not something that happens often. In this place of prayer, God can make you to feel the pain of the person you are praying for.

Prayer has been the starting place for any and all growth in my life, both personal and business. It has shifted my entire perspective on who I thought I was versus who God created me to be. Prayer has centered me and grounded me in truth—God's truth. I'm no longer easily moved by the words of others or the stressors of life because prayer has brought about an inner calmness I never imagined. Now I start and end my day with prayer. There is always a constant dialogue going on with me and God. I love asking Him:

- What are you trying to show me, God?

- What do you want me to do in this situation?

- How can I be a blessing, God?

- Give me clear direction in this area, Father.

I am always engaging God in every aspect of my life, and He is showing up so strong.

OBEDIENCE

God has a reason why He gives us the unction to pray at certain times. The Word says, "And I sought for a man among them, that should make up the hedge and stand in the gap before me for the land, that I should not destroy it: but I found none" (Ezekiel 22:30).

I know that whenever God is impressing on me to pray, there is definitely a good reason. One night God woke me up out of my sleep to pray. Since I did not know what to pray, I prayed in tongues because I understood that God knew what and how He wanted me to pray. I prayed in tongues until the weight of prayer lifted. I later found out that a family member was contemplating suicide at the same time I began to pray, and God aborted the plans of the enemy to take her life.

In Genesis, we read that Abraham was trying to talk God out of destroying Sodom and Gomorrah, but God could find no one to pray for them. Abraham negotiated with God from finding fifty people all the way down to ten—that if He (God) could find at least ten people to pray on behalf of the city, He would not destroy it. And we all know how that ended. The city was destroyed because God could find no one to stand in prayer to overcome the works and the plans of the enemy (see Genesis 18).

I have settled in my spirit that I want to be the one God calls on to stand in the gap for families, communities, nations, churches, and whatever God wants to have birthed in prayer in the earth. Would you join me in this commitment to pray?

PRAYING AMISS

You ask and do not receive, because you ask amiss, that you may spend it on your pleasures" (James 4:3 NKJV). Sometimes we pray, and we never see answers to our prayers. There are reasons why:

- You pray without faith (Mark 11:23–24).

- You do not pray according to the will of God, which is the Word of God (1 John 5:14).

- You pray selfishly (James 4:3).

- You pray with unforgiveness (Mark 11:25–26).

The Bible has laid out the principles by which, if we adhere to them, our prayers would constantly be answered. It is our duty as Christians to find out what they are. If your prayers are not answered, it is not because God does not like answering your prayers. On the contrary, He desires so much that we commune with Him daily. It is because we are often not adhering to the principles already laid out for us concerning prayer.

We pray amiss because we have not been taught how to structure our prayers for proven results. Often we pray out of the will of God. This principle of praying according to His will is essential to having answered prayers because if we are praying out of our soulish desires (our mind, will, and emotions), we are praying amiss. We must continue to renew our minds in the Word of God so we receive the mind of Christ on every issue. Once our will gets superimposed with the will of God, then our prayers are well on their way to heavenly approval.

We also pray amiss because we don't pray by the Word of God. It says angels hearken to the *voice* of the Word of God (see Psalm 103:20), which essentially means our angels are on standby listening for the Word of God to come forth from our mouths. The moment you release a prayer formulated by the Word of God, the angels move quickly to perform it on your behalf. Our prayers go unanswered because we all perish for lack of knowledge, as stated in the Word. It's time we begin to study to understand exactly what is available to us when we pray.

WARFARE TONGUES

I call this a shift in the way we speak in tongues. It is more aggressive and more authoritative. It is a place in prayer where you're violently taking your victory by force (see Matthew 11:12).

The weight of the Lord comes upon me to do this. Others call it "the spirit of prayer," some call it an "impression on your spirit to pray," and some call it "a burden in the Spirit." Usually I pray until the weight lifts. The timing of the weight or burden lifting depends on the Holy Spirit. It could be thirty minutes or two hours, but it depends on the Holy Spirit. Once the weight lifts, then I know that everything is good. You can go on about your day after that because you know you've done what the Lord wanted you to do.

BEST TIMES TO PRAY

My best time to pray is at five in the morning. I am not a morning person, so this is extremely difficult for me; however, God is always asking me to seek Him early. I even asked, "God, what time do You want me to do my devotion and my communion with You?" and He said, "5 a.m." Imagine that. Why wouldn't He instead say 5 p.m.? But as I studied the Word of God, I realized that major things happened when God's people prayed early. Battles were won when they arose early and prayed. Courses were shifted and disaster was averted when they prayed early. "O Lord, in the morning you hear my voice; in the morning I prepare a sacrifice for you and watch" (Psalm 5:3 ESV). "I love them that love me; and those that seek me early shall find me" (Proverbs 8:17).

God also wakes me up at other specific times to pray as He so wills. I have missed it at times because I'm tired, but for the most part, I try to honor God with His requests for me to pray.

Mastering Wisdom

Solomon asked God for wisdom, and God answered him and blessed him with wisdom (see 1 Kings 3:5–13). Solomon amassed an enormous amount of wealth, influence, prosperity, and abundance as a result of God's wisdom being given to him; so essentially, wealth is a by-product of wisdom. In the same way, the Holy Spirit led me to begin to pray for wisdom. Wisdom can give you access to wealth. The Bible says, "Wisdom is the principal thing;

therefore get wisdom" (Proverbs 4:7). Wisdom is needed. It helps you to make the right choices in life and to make the right connections.

When you have the supernatural wisdom of God, you have everything. I remember when God told me to invest in a particular mutual fund. I had no idea why at the time, but I felt compelled to put all of my retirement funds into it. It was so random and bizarre that even the investment officers kept calling me and asking me why I invested in this extremely aggressive fund. Also, better yet, why did I put *all* of my money in that particular fund? Unusual, right? Uncommon? It surely was, but my decision to use that uncommon investment strategy was the sole reason I had enough money to start our business. If I had not followed God's specific instruction, I would have missed a very rare opportunity to seal our legacy and to leave an inheritance for our children. "A good man leaves an inheritance to his children's children" (Proverbs 13:22 NKJV).

The Word of God also says that God gives seed to the sower (2 Corinthians 9:10). What if I had discarded my seed? What if I had not recognized the seed God had given me as something to invest and multiply but instead had squandered it? I would not have had what I needed when the door of opportunity arose. I believe this happens to many of us, more often than not. We live for the now and not for the hope of tomorrow. Most people think *You only live once, so let's splurge it all!* not realizing that financial opportunities will arise and those without the wisdom of planting for multiplication will be disappointed later. This is why most people live check to check. They never delay gratification.

Wisdom has shown me to let every dollar I earn work for me at least twice as hard as when I made it. This is how wealth is created. Remember the parable of the talents?

The Parable of the Talents

It will be like a man going on a journey, who called his servants and entrusted to them his property. To one he gave five talents, to another two, to another one, to each according to his ability. Then he went away. ...
Now after a long time the master of those servants came and settled accounts with them. And he ... who had received the one talent came forward, saying, 'Master, I knew you to be a hard man, reaping where you did not sow, and gathering where you scattered no seed, so I was

afraid, and I went and hid your talent in the ground. Here, you have what is yours.' But his master answered him, 'You wicked and slothful servant! You knew that I reap where I have not sown and gather where I scattered no seed? Then you ought to have invested my money with the bankers, and at my coming I should have received what was my own with interest. So take the talent from him and give it to him who has the ten talents.

For to everyone who has will more be given, and he will have an abundance. But from the one who has not, even what he has will be taken away. And cast the worthless servant into the outer darkness. In that place there will be weeping and gnashing of teeth.'"

- Matthew 25:14-30 ESV

The guy who had only one talent buried his talent and did not invest it to where it yielded some type of increase, so God sent him to hell, and he was referred to as worthless. I believe this is the way each of us will be evaluated at the end of our lives by God. He'll ask, "What did you do with the resources, the money, the gifts, and the talents I gave you?

- How did you multiply them?

- How were they beneficial to someone else's life?

- Did you sit on your talents, skills, and opportunities, or did you make the crossover from being a consumer to being a producer."

I really believe God is going to ask us one day, "Did you multiply anything I gave you? Anything? Why not? You had everything you needed to create wealth, so why didn't you produce and multiply what you produced?" This is why wisdom is the principle thing.

STEAL AWAY TIME WITH THE FATHER

My husband asked me to go with him golfing one morning, and although my heart wanted to say yes, I couldn't because God, too, was tugging on my heart to spend time with Him. Although it was a good thing to want to be with my husband, it was the right thing to pull back to spend time with God. It doesn't happen always, but when it does, I encourage you to steal away time to be with the Father.

God then gave me a glimpse of planting needed seeds inside me. What He showed me was so amazing and so mind-blowing that I knew only He could do it in my life. The Father wanted to drag me into another dimension of grace and abundance and increase so I could be a storehouse for His kingdom. Yes, me! I'm *so* glad I answered His call that day. He downloaded strategies and direction and plans for my future.

Wouldn't you like to know a thing before it begins? That's the advantage we have as believers. God will show us a thing before it is authenticated and manifested in the earth so that when it happens, only God gets the glory.

Just like He talks to me, He wants to speak to you too. But are you listening and obeying His call? Are you so bombarded by distractions that you wouldn't know the voice of God if it hit you with a Mack truck? Well, there's good news. It's not too late. Let today be the day you separate yourself to give God the time out of your day He deserves. I promise you, you won't be disappointed. I wasn't.

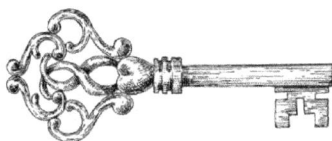

— 6 —

THE POWER OF PURPOSE AND WISDOM

Take your seat

PURPOSE IS WHAT GOD HAS CREATED YOU TO DO on the earth. It's the thing only you can do with excellence. This is why the competition thing is not necessary in the kingdom. Think about it like this:

We are all pieces to a puzzle in the kingdom of God. There is no other puzzle piece like me, and although others may try, they will never be able to quite fit in place the way I can because I was designed specifically for something no one else can do quite like me. My life is a fingerprint of God. Each person has his or her unique identity, just like a fingerprint—no two are alike. But the enemy and errored thinking has caused many of us to think narrow-mindedly about these things. This thinking is a trick of the enemy to keep us fighting among ourselves when we have all been given an opportunity for a seat at the table. You only have to get in position to receive the invitation.

Purpose should be your driving force. Once you establish what your purpose is, you can rule a lot of things out that were basic chatter. You can laser focus your life. Purpose is an essential discovery process; anything outside of it should be secondary. Understanding your purpose will help you make the right decisions in your life—you'll know when to say yes and when to say no. I always had a problem with saying no. I wanted to help people. I found myself in situations where I felt depleted because I was all over the place. Once I got clear about my purpose, saying no wasn't a problem for me anymore. Now I'm clear about what I need to be doing at any given time.

God has a purpose and a plan for each of our lives. "I knew you before I formed you in your mother's womb" (Jeremiah 1:5 NLT). It's time we get about the business of figuring out what that is and move in that direction.

VISION

Vision is the big picture that helps you to see what you are aiming for in life. Vision can be revealed when we allow our imaginations to run wild with possibility, to dream again. In doing that, we expose ourselves to options, options we never had when the limitations of our mind held us captive in the pits of mediocrity or even substandard lifestyles.

Purpose and vision are connected; however, purpose fine-tunes your focus in life. If you know your purpose is to do a certain thing, then you can say no to a whole lot of other unnecessary things. Identifying your purpose is the most strategic thing you can do to jet-set your life. It'll send you directly into launch mode because a lot of people who live without knowing what their purpose is are kind of like the little hamster on the wheel that's constantly running around and around, never getting anywhere. They are not focused on their place of purpose.

For example, if you don't know all the capabilities your iPhone has, you talk to the creator of the phone. Imagine having an iPhone and not knowing you have Siri. In the same way, it's important to seek our creator—God—about our purpose.

- What am I created for?

- What was I put on the earth to do?

I didn't know I could be a public speaker. I didn't know I was called to business. I didn't know I was to be a multimillionaire. I didn't know I had enough in me to pour out to other people. I didn't know I should be a nurse practitioner. I just didn't know.

What you think about yourself is usually something totally different than what God thinks about you. That's why your purpose is imperative to figure out. If you could just focus on that, then it will get you leaps and bounds ahead in life.

I believe that many times our lives are often positively affected by what I would like to call "pointers"—people God has placed in our lives to assist us in pointing our purpose out to us. Consequently, this helps us to steer our lives in the right direction. Pointers lightly tap you on the shoulder and say, "Your purpose is in that direction." I'm not at all suggesting you allow negative complainers to dictate who God has created you to be, or allow people to condemn you or make you feel in any way ashamed of being you. God's pointers tell you who you are because they see what's inside you. My hair stylist said out of the blue one day, "You're a very influential person," and I was like, "What are you talking about? Where did that come from? We were just having a regular conversation." She said, "No, I don't think you understand. You're very influential, and people need to hear from you." *What is she talking about?* I just could not get it. But she was putting seeds inside me about who I was. I didn't even see what she saw. And then even other people would say, "Well, you know you're influential; people will come to hear you or to be a part of whatever you are doing. You draw people." And I'd be like, "What are you talking about?" I had no idea what any of them were talking about. One reason is I'd never even considered doing meetings, conferences, or events I'd have to invite anyone to. The thought had literally never crossed my mind. But when God sends one person after another to say the same thing about you, you begin to notice a pattern. *Are you trying to tell me something, God?*

When you have the right people around you, they will begin to expose qualities, talents, and strengths you never imagined you had inside. This is why the right connections and relationships matter. Pay very close attention to who you are keeping company with. Who's in your ear? Who are you allowing airtime in your life? Because words have power! They will either uplift and encourage you or they will slowly chip away at your soul and tear you down completely. Surround yourself with people who walk with God and have His spirit. Surround yourself with encouragers. Surround yourself with motivators. I assure you, if you do this, every dynamic of your life will change for the better. There is no doubt about it.

Although pointers will show you the way to purpose, God alone will confirm it to you. Sometimes God will use people to release a prophetic word that gives you clear insight to your purpose. Other times God may just give you an inner witness or a deep knowing that settles the matter in your heart. God can also speak audibly to you. No matter how God chooses to identify your purpose, just lean into the process because it's necessary. God is the source in which all questions can be answered about your life.

- What should I be when I grow up?

- Should I go to college or should I start my own business?

- Who should I marry?

- Is this a person I should stay connected to or not?

- Where should I work?

- What church should I attend?

- What books should I read?

God has all the answers. He alone can reveal every little detail to you. The best part about it is that He won't allow you to miss it when you trust Him and obey His instruction.

I was sitting at a table one night at a Bible study at someone's home, and the leader said to the group, "Okay, let's share what your purpose is."

All those at the table said what their purpose was. I was forty at the time, and when they got to me, I had no idea what I was called to do. I had no idea where my place of purpose was. I felt embarrassed and inadequate in a lot of ways at just not being able to verbally say what my purpose was. This moment was majorly impactful to my life because what it made me realize was that I was cruising through life without a GPS, almost like wandering around, so to speak. I was doing a lot of things, but none of them was what I was called to do. I had settled my life into a good ol' routine. I'm sure most of you have experienced it before. You know when you go to work, get off work, and go back again. I was doing the same ol' thing day after day after day with no fulfillment whatsoever.

I've heard a lot of people, even celebrities, say that when you find your purpose, you wake up excited. You don't drag in. You don't think to yourself *I wish I didn't have to go to work today.* You're just motivated to do the thing you love to do. It's no longer a job. It's an opportunity. It's a life mission. It's your purpose! Well, at that time I hadn't reached that place, and I had to cry out to God for answers. "I'm forty years old. I need to know what my purpose is. I have no idea what it is, and I need you to tell me specifically what it is so I can get about the business of doing it." If I had been more focused, it would have taken less time, but it took me about three months of pleading with God for Him to tell me what my purpose was. I was waiting and praying to Him and just saying, "Can you reveal to me who I am? Who am I?"

It took about three months for Him to finally tell me who I was and who He has called me to be. I journaled everything He told me, and there are places in my journal where I put question marks. "Are you saying I'm called to do *this?* What?" and He'd confirm I'd heard Him. He would send people to even confirm what He'd told me was inside me. It broke me down every time because they were validating who I really was.

ENLARGING YOUR CAPACITY

I think it's important to identify your self-imposed limitations. When you hone in to these mind blocks, you can enlarge your ability to receive more from God.

Let's say you have a business opportunity, a partnership, or an ownership in a business. Your mind might be limited on the *how* or logistics.

Perhaps you don't have enough financial resources and are living beneath your financial means. Your mind can't grasp the principle of ownership. When I talk about enlarging the capacity of what you can receive, you have to see it God's way first. If you don't see yourself a certain way, if you don't see yourself as an owner, if you don't see yourself debt free, if you don't see yourself set free, healed, and delivered, or if you don't see yourself married, then that will impact your life.

REAL ESTATE

I have always been passionate about real estate. When I first started hearing God's voice, He used my experience in real estate to train me how to navigate it in the Spirit.

My husband and I would buy a house and move into it every two years. We were constantly moving because of his job. I was very frustrated with the things that happened in the buying process and with the agent on the last house, the house we're staying in now. It was a horrible situation. Through this, though, I became passionate about real estate. I wound up becoming a real estate agent but quickly found out it entailed too much and was not for me. I worked for a few months, but in the end I realized I wasn't called to do it. I was called to real estate but as an owner and developer. I was right in following the path of real estate and getting the knowledge base but wrong in the method on which I went about it. It led me further into purpose.

You'll never be what you can't see in your mind. It says in the Word, "As [a man] thinketh in his heart, so is he" (Proverbs 23:7). When you enlarge your capacity to receive, you get more revelation about who God has created you to be and how to stretch your mind into living truer to that. Whatever you think is the biggest thing in your life that you'll do, then just think bigger. What God has planned for you to do is bigger than your wildest imagination.

For you to be able to fulfill your purpose, you have to renew your mind with the Word. God told Jeremiah he had been called as a prophet to the nations, to root out and to pull down, to destroy, to build and plant (see Jeremiah 1:10). Jeremiah's mind could not fathom the capacity of his assignment until God helped him see it.

To enlarge your capacity, you have to renew your mind in the Word so as to be able to grasp the plan of God concerning you.

History has it that Jeremiah fulfilled his destiny once he accepted his purpose with his mind. His prophecies over the years were fulfilled. The nations that were pulled down, destroyed, built, and planted had all those things happen according to the prophecies of this young man. Why? He enlarged his capacity to receive the plan of God for him.

Before you can enlarge your capacity, you need to identify the limitations in your mind. If you don't see yourself debt free, you will never be debt free. If you don't see yourself married, you may never be married. The Bible says you are the person you see yourself as (see Proverbs 23:7). You need to see it in the eye of your mind before you can possess it. This is why Romans 12:2 is very important to every believer: "And be not conformed to this world: but be ye transformed by the renewing of your mind, that ye may prove what is that good, and acceptable, and perfect, will of God."

If God says you are rich, you need to see that reality with the eye of your mind before it can come to pass in you. In my home, we have what we call vision days. We drive around certain neighborhoods to see things we wouldn't normally see. We get pictures of what we like, and this helps in stretching our mind-set and imagination.

STEPS TO TAKE TO MASTER YOUR PURPOSE

SEEK GOD ALWAYS, AND HE WILL ORDER YOUR STEPS.

I'm always in conversation with God about which things I can improve upon. Seeking God diligently is the first and foremost thing to do. Develop a close relationship with God, or just begin to seek God about who you are and who He's created you to be. It's valuable. I've learned God is displeased about the reach of His kingdom because many of us in the body of Christ are *not in position.* We don't know how to do business. We don't have the wealth, influence, connections, or things needed to further the gospel. We don't have what we should have by now to meet the needs of the general church body.

God is trying to shift us into positions of power in the earth. We don't see much going on because we're just not in place in the kingdom. It's off balance, and everybody's looking at everybody else to fix the problems. Everybody has a complaint but no solutions. It's time for us all to take our positions, our proper positions, in the kingdom of God. It's time to overtake the enemy in this earth because right now it's a bunch of craziness that's going on.

STUDY AND IMPROVE YOUR KNOWLEDGE BASE ON ANYTHING ASSOCIATED WITH YOUR PURPOSE.

If you are called to be a mentor, study everything that entails. Put things in place to prepare for your calling or the next step so that when time and chance meet, you can capture the opportunity. You'll be ready; you won't miss it.

PRACTICE, PRACTICE, PRACTICE.

What you continuously do, you will begin to master. Les Brown has a story about practicing his radio pitch. When the time came for his opportunity, he sounded like a real professional because he had practiced and perfected his craft when no one was watching or listening. Study and practice the things you are called to in order to improve your performance.

VISION DAYS

As well as driving around nice neighborhoods with multimillion-dollar houses on our vision days, we go on vacations to see different cultures and environments. You don't know what you want until you've seen it. You have to get a picture of what that looks like. I'm amazed with people who say, "Well, I don't like that," but they've never tried it. You've got to stretch your capacity, and sometimes you can only do that by seeing and being around different things. How can you say you don't like a woman if you've never met her, or a man if you're not in relationship with him? You can't take somebody else's opinion about it. All this stretches your capacity to receive more from God. It's the power of visualizing your future, or seeing yourself in the future.

A major thing for me is that even when I get visions about people, if I can see it in my mind's eye, it's already done. I've always been very visual. If you have dreams about going to the beach, then you need to imagine yourself breathing and smelling the salty air, walking into the water, and hearing the sounds of the ocean because then one day you can do that very thing you're envisioning.

I told my husband, "I want to go to the Kentucky Derby." I just made that statement. He asked why. I didn't know why. I just thought it was pretty cool. I wanted to have one of those big hats on and look cute and check it out. The very next year, we got an invitation to attend the Derby. I knew this was God. I said the desires of my heart out loud and ended up with exactly that. I saw myself being there too. Talk about visualization. Mike got a corporate, all-expenses-paid trip to the Kentucky Derby. They picked us up from the airport in a limo. We got placed at the hotel with all the stars. I saw Shaq walking down the hallway. We passed him, Anthony Anderson, Star Jones, Scottie Pippin, Gary Peyton, and other major celebrities in our hotel. It was amazing.

I knew God was trying to show us where we were supposed to be. Mike said, "Girl, you are crazy." But those ten or so limos lined up at the front of the hotel were there to take *all of us*—those of us who had the corporate invite—to the Kentucky Derby. We were in corporate row. We had the best seats, free food laid out; it was a top-of-the-line experience. We had a police car escort us. It was almost like we were President Barack Obama and Michelle or something. God was showing me we were always supposed to live like this. I told my husband this was something we could never have planned ourselves or done in our own strength.

We were hanging out with millionaires and multimillionaires *before* acquiring our business. They had no idea we were just regular people, and they probably didn't care, for that matter. It's only God who can put you in position to see things He's trying to pull out of you. Mike and I were walking down the hallway of the hotel, and this lady was pointing at me saying, "I know her, I know her." Mike said, "I think she thinks you are somebody." I said, "Yeah, because I *am* somebody. She'd better keep looking."

It was one of those moments when God gave me a wink in my life and said, "You know, you're valuable to me, and I'm going to open doors for you, special doors. I want to treat you with lovingkindness and put you in a place and seat you in a position I called you to be in, one you feel you're not even worthy enough to have. But because I love you, and you're my daughter and you're special to me, I'm exposing you to this; I'm going to give this to you." Even in those moments, I see God.

— 7 —

GOAL SETTING

Keep moving forward

I LIVE MY LIFE BASED ON purpose, vision, and goals. Along with God, these are the driving forces in my life that help me to actualize what I've visualized. While vision is the big picture of what your end goal is, goals are actionable steps to get to the big picture, the vision, or the place of purpose. Goals, for me, strategically break down what needs to happen to get you from one destination to another. You need to set short-term goals, long-term goals, and even daily, weekly, quarterly, five-year, ten-year, and even 30-year goals. Most people don't get past five-year goals.

Ten- and twenty-year projections are good, too because the Word of God says if you lack vision, you perish (Proverbs 29:18). Vision is something we should always keep ahead of us and strive—not strive, I shouldn't use that language—but you should always be trying to get to that place of vision. You should always be setting up goals to move you from one position to the next. If you don't set goals, then you'll wake up a week, two weeks, later with the same unaccomplished thing on your to-do list. I've found that by setting these goals, I see my life moving forward, and I'm guided by God and the divine wisdom He has given me by setting them.

How to Set Goals:

When I knew I needed to go back to school, I set goals toward that which helped me tremendously, and I became a nurse practitioner in two years.

- I looked up schools and institutions that would let me accomplish my goal of being a nurse practitioner in the shortest time.

- I checked for the one that would give me the fewest number of classes to take in the shortest amount of time.

PURPOSEFUL JOURNALING

Capture conversations with God

JOURNALING IS A PROPHETIC ACTION. It has been a very important part of my life because it's shifted how I see the world. As I look through my journals over the years, I often start crying as I see how God has been leading me. By incorporating this step daily, He's been telling me everything before it actually happens.

When God gives you a word, He gives you a download. It comes fast, and it's fleeting. If you don't capture it and write it down or document it, you're going to lose it because the Word of God says the enemy comes immediately to steal the word. I realized it was important for me to document the things I heard and thought because my God-thoughts always bring a moment of healing on the inside to get me better.

My goal in life is to always be a better version of myself each day. I think about it.

> *Am I better than I was yesterday?* And if I am, I am off to a good start. Journaling has helped me to evaluate many things.
> *Have I achieved this?*
> *Am I a good person?*
> *Are the things I'm saying hurtful or helpful to people?*
> *Are people being encouraged around me?*
> *What does my life look like?*

Journaling is a place where I can write all my feelings down without being judged or feeling bad about myself. It is an avenue to release pain and fear, and it's healing for me. Secondly, I have found out God speaks to me in my writing. As I said before, whenever I would set myself to pray, I would hear God say, "Get your pen."

He once told me I was called to preach the gospel. I thought, *I know that can't be God. I don't want to preach to anybody at the church because those church people are so religious.* I had seen the backside of what people see when leaders preach and perform. When I saw myself teaching in a church, I identified that with *Oh no, I don't ever want to work in a church; that's the worst thing ever.* But all along, God was leading me to that place.

From my journaling, I was able to see how God was telling me to get ready, this was coming. He told me somebody was going to call me about a leadership role and that it was okay for me to take it. When I did get the call, I'd totally forgotten about it. Journaling is valuable to capture those moments with God because you're always hearing from God but don't remember it, and then He doesn't get the glory. He could have answered a prayer you would have forgotten about had you not journaled. Journaling is invaluable. It can also be a testimony about how we can hear God's voice when a lot of people think we don't.

HOW TO INCORPORATE JOURNALING IN YOUR LIFE

People often ask me how they can begin journaling in their own lives. To start, you should take baby steps. For instance, say for one whole week, *I am going to journal.* If you don't set a goal for writing, you may not be able to keep up with doing it. At the end of each day, take about fifteen minutes of quiet time to think about everything that occurred. Write what your day was about, the things you were impacted by, your feelings about what happened that could have gone better. What should you have done? What should you not have done? Recapturing your day at the end of the day refocuses your mind because it helps you to see things more clearly without the emotion. For instance, *I shouldn't have reacted like that in that conversation. I could do better next time.* It helps you reevaluate and process. Fifteen minutes before bed is a good time for a strategic release that allows you to deal with the issues of your heart. The enemy is always looking for an opportunity to create offense in our hearts. If you don't release it, it will fester. Most people don't talk about it out of their mouths but will do so in the form of reflection. Molehills turn into mountains when you don't deal with those things.

God is giving us insight and direction when we sleep, therefore it's important to brain dump to release anything that may keep you bound. Before you go to sleep, you should always intend to forgive any offense, no matter if you're right or wrong. This a way to ensure peace. Just give all of your concerns to God. Surrender everything to Him and He will perfect that which concerns you (Psalms 138:8 NKJV). After you have allowed your mind to get clear, then expect God to speak to you in your dreams. "In a dream, in a vision of the night, when deep sleep falleth upon men, in slumberings upon the bed; then he openeth the ears of men, and sealeth their instruction" (Job 33:15–16 NKJV).

The fact that the Bible was recorded and documented by someone for our use today is revelational; so we, too, must journal and document our legacies, revelations, prayers, and journeys for the next generation. Learning from our past experiences will teach them to be overcomers. We can't keep it all to ourselves. We must share what we have learned with others.

Mornings are great for commanding my day. I journal my dreams or any revelation God gave me over the night to capture important messages and instruction from Him. In the night, I use the journal as a moment of self-reflection. I evaluate my day and try to figure out what things I could have said, done, or responded to differently. Then I journal and write about those things specifically. I write how certain moments in my day made me feel, and then I force myself to process why it made me feel that way. This is a time to let go of all offenses before you close your eyes because the enemy will use offense to steal your joy in every way. Relationships and families are dismantled because of offense. Bitterness, offense, guilt, trauma, and shame creep into your mind and lay a foundation of sickness and disease if not properly dealt with.

Journaling is cathartic and healing for your soul and your body. It is God's way of formulating a means of release.

Journaling has been a source of great peace in my life. I often go back and review the level of insight God gave me and think to myself, *Wow, God is amazing.* Just the other day, I looked over about six of my journals and realized God was leading me the entire way. He was telling me of things to come, giving me insight into the future and instructions about decision-making and overall clear direction. I began to sob at the evidence of the hand of God on my life on the pages. It was

astounding. This is why journaling is so imperative.

Oftentimes, you might have prayed about
something, and God answered it, but because you
didn't journal it, you forgot. The Word says Satan
comes immediately to steal the Word of God (see
Mark 4:14-16). Have you ever noticed how fast
you forget a dream you had the night before if you
don't write it down? The enemy does not want you
grabbing hold of revelation of the Lord and allowing it to grow in your heart because then you are
a force to be reckoned with. So he steals the Word
quickly from you. The same thing happens in
church when you have a good message—you leave
church, and someone asks how good church was
that day. Then they ask what the message was
about. You really have to think hard. *What in the
world did the preacher teach on?* That's the enemy
again, trying to steal breakthrough moments
away from you. This is why meditating on the
Word of God is so important.

Journaling has been a source of healing in my
marriage, friendships, and even in our business.
God begins to open new avenues of revelation in
the act of journaling. Some of the wealthiest and

most influential people journal. Pay attention! There is always a roadmap to success if you pay attention to the details.

IMPORTANCE OF SELF-REFLECTION

Self-reflection is about evaluating who you are and what you're projecting to the world. How do people see you? It's not getting into a place of trying to please everyone but evaluating who you want to be. Most times we're not fully at the place where we want to be because we see other aspects of people. I know I do. I may look at a person and think, *I love the joy she has inside. She's just bubbly.* You know how you see those bubbly people— they're perky and happy, and you wish you had a little bit of that. Then you might see somebody strong and bold, and you may want a part of that. You look at different aspects of people that you want for yourself. My pastor always says success leaves clues, and when you self-reflect, you can also look at pieces of yourself that are not where they should be. Then you can take good things you see in other people and try to emulate those things (but not to the point of comparison because people get caught up in comparison).

I hope I'm communicating effectively on this point because I don't want people to compare themselves to others. What I am saying is, how can you add this formula to your life to improve in a particular area? For example, if I see someone bold, I may even question him or her. I would talk to people who were good at public speaking and say, "What is it that got you to this place? Where did it come from? Were you always good at it?" If they had fears, then I would say, "How did you overcome your fears?" Then I would take what they learned and apply it to my life.

When you're doing your self-reflection, it pulls out things you wouldn't normally see about your-self, and it puts it in front of you; then you have to deal with it. It doesn't stay hidden. That's the goal. Because what you leave hidden grows into some-thing much worse. That's why it's important to self-reflect, to always be constantly and actively working to grow into everything God has made you to be.

— 9 —

FEAR, THE DREAM ASSASSINATOR

Don't be held captive

FEAR IS A DREAM ASSASSINATOR. The enemy uses it to create boundaries between you and your destiny. It camouflages your place of purpose. Fear grounds your feet and stops them from moving into your God-ordained purpose. Fear is a reckless spirit of destruction. Fear's chief desire is to destroy any and all potential. It is the destroyer of what could be, what was meant to be, and what is.

Fear either paralyzes or it operates in patterns and cycles of familiarity. Fear allows you to hold a banner of mediocrity proudly in hopes that potential won't get a peek of what true greatness looks like inside you. It allows word curses to trample through your mind with such freedom and liberty that purpose and vision can never be exposed.

Fear holds purpose and vision captive, and fear's goal is to keep you trapped in a cycle of defeat so you will never realize you were intended for greater things.

When people first asked me to speak, I would always say, "Why do you all keep doing that?" When I told people I was afraid of public speaking, they would look at me like, *Are you serious?* They could not see it. I like to be in the background. I'll help you on a project, but I don't want to run the project; I don't want to be the head on it. I was also fearful of leadership roles. I can do a leadership role in my career, but outside of that, whenever people would ask me to lead or head something up, I would always say, "No I'm not doing it. I'm not signing up for that."

There was a project at work where we mentioned the fears and the strengths of each other. Everybody who gave me three of my strengths said things like, "You're a great leader," "You're an excellent leader," "You're going to be a leader." It's funny how the people around you can tell you who you are, but you don't even see the qualities in yourself.

Two years ago, a woman asked me to be a speaker for a girls' event. I said to her, "Why would you even think I can speak?" She answered, "I don't know. God told me to ask you." And I said, "No, absolutely not. I'm not going to do it, but I'll call my cousin because she's a good speaker; let me get her to speak at your event." I gave her a reference.

Then the following year she came right back and asked the same question. I said, "Didn't I tell you last year I'm not a speaker? I don't speak in front of people." But this was the year I'd told God I was going to say yes more; I was going to lean more into things I felt He wanted me to do. When I was journaling that day, God said, "She's coming back to ask you to speak again." When she came back, I looked at her, squinted my eyes, and said,

"I'll do it, sure, since you keep asking. You're relentless." I ended up speaking at her conference last year, and I had forty-five minutes. I thought I would have nothing to say. The host had to tell me, "Tonya, you only have six minutes left." Wow, and I had much more to give. I was nervous, but once I got up there and started speaking, it went better than I'd anticipated.

Much of the time people think the status of their lives is a result of somebody else's actions or external factors. If they don't have enough money good relationships, or they feel all alone (or whatever the problem may be in their lives), they feel it is somebody else's fault they are the way they are. Most times nobody else is to blame for you being in the position you are now. *You* are your problem.

We're our own worst enemy because we never think the best of ourselves. We under-qualify ourselves most times, and in doing that, we stop the flow of God moving in our lives. God has placed many gifts in me to empower me to teach and train women and to entrust them with the knowledge of things I've learned; but if I centered my whole life around not doing any public speaking, keeping it all to myself and not sharing it with people on a larger scale, I'd be doing a disservice to God and His kingdom. I'd set this boundary in my life out of fear, and it was stunting my growth.

We don't look at ourselves the way God looks at us. We see our lives through such a small lens. We underestimate every aspect of our lives, and it's not until God begins to renew our minds that we come into a place of being able to break off that whole mind-set of "stinking thinking."

MEDIOCRITY

I allowed mediocrity to seep into my family. I raised my kids and did not set high standards for them. My mom's goal for me was to at least get a C, so anytime I got at least C or above, she was okay with that. I was later frustrated by that, so I told my children passing was good, but we always gave them incentives to get at least an average grade. They never pushed themselves, and I never pushed them to push themselves, but I wanted them to want more from themselves.

Everybody is not meant to get a bachelor's or master's degree, as it may not be a priority. I know multimillionaires with no education who are successful, so I thought maybe I could encourage my kids to be entrepreneurial by giving them good role models. We focused on Robert Kiyosaki, the author of *Rich Dad, Poor Dad*. We purchased his Cash Flow game to help them understand how money is a tool, not a master, and that it's not about how much money you make but rather about what you do with the money you keep. We also tried to instill financial principles to them based on godly principles, and mainly the truth that "neither he who plants is anything, nor he who waters, but God who gives the increase" (1 Corinthians 3:7 NKJV).

I tried to give our kids the things I had to struggle for, things I never got, but in doing that, I realized I was crippling them. If I could change anything about my parenting, I would let my kids fail more. I never let them fail. I would see them trying to do something, and if they couldn't do it, I would help them. They never developed the problem-solving skills they needed to master things in life.

Failure is a gift. It causes you to refocus and make adjustments on things that didn't work before. You can improve on those things you tried before and failed at: you can make better choices;

you can see which route not to take because of the bad results in choosing it before. You might have tried something one way before, but later you can come back and do it a totally different way because of the lessons of failure.

Failure is not something that should be feared. It should be embraced. A lot of times we are afraid of failure; it paralyzes most people. That's what I dealt with often in life—fear of failure. Because I feared failure, I never did anything. But now I see that failure is a gift.

MASTERING MENTAL BLOCKS

A mental block is a firm boundary you set up in your mind that makes you unable to get to a higher level in your life. It can be a form of fear that limits your mind. God can tell you to do something, but your mental block will inform you you are not qualified to do it. Take, for instance, Moses. Initially when God asked him to go to Egypt and deliver His people, Moses's mental block prevented him from seeing what God was seeing in him—he thought he wasn't qualified enough to be a deliverer.

A mental block can also look like low self-esteem—not knowing who you are and not taking responsibility of that. Low self-esteem can cripple you, and if you're viewing yourself as the opposite of what God has created you to be, you're living a substandard lifestyle. You may be functional and have things, but your level of living is still substandard to the level of living of your calling. You might not even think you're capable of doing that thing God has told you to do because these thoughts are circling your mind: *I'm not good enough, I'm not worthy enough, I don't deserve this, I don't have enough money to fund this,* or *I don't have enough ability or physical ability to do this thing.*

Getting clear on issues in your heart, in your mind, and in your emotions—broken places that have occurred because of life experience or trauma—is crucial. Those things need to be settled for you to get a clear knowledge of who you are and break that old thinking pattern so you can soar beyond these boundaries. Wash out the boundaries you put in your mind about who you are, and being able to do this starts with having a high self-esteem.

I haven't hit the pinnacle of life—at least, I don't think I'm there. I don't think anybody will ever get there because we always need to continue to learn, to continue to adjust, to continue to grow. Life is going to be constantly evolving, but we should always be getting better than we were yesterday, not worse.

You should always be moving forward. If you find yourself moving back, you need to settle down, regroup, reevaluate. Do the work. Whatever the work is you need to do, do that work that helps you continue forward; we need to always be moving forward, not backward.

HOW TO BOOST YOUR MENTALITY

- Study and meditate on the Word.

- Speak positive confessions about yourself out loud. Create confessions grounded in the Word of God. Example: "I have an abundance of wisdom. Wisdom is always available to me. No matter the circumstance, I have the supernatural wisdom of God and I always know exactly what to do" (James 1:5).

- Record yourself saying positive things about who you are. for example: "I am bold! I am confident! I am more than a conqueror! I am strong! I am wealthy! I am a leader! I am fearless!" It's not what someone says about you, it's what you believe about yourself that matters. Train yourself to believe positive things about who you are.

- Read books on positive thinking and the power of the right mind-set. How you see the world and the things in it will sculpt your life. Your thought process is painting the canvas of your life. Do you like the picture staring back at you?

— 10 —

THE POWER OF CONFESSION

See things happen

CONFESSION IS A STATEMENT OF FAITH in something you believe in. You're producing your words on this belief. There's power in your words. There's power in your confession. Most people don't understand this power. They make confessions or say things about their lives every day, and they just don't realize what they're saying. I was doing this too. Whatever I was saying out of my mouth I was producing in my life. The Holy Spirit showed me my language needed to change. He even told me, "Your tongue is an unruly member, and it must be contained."

> Death and life are in the power of the tongue, and those who love it and indulge it will eat its fruit and bear the consequences of their words.
> —Proverbs 18:21 AMP

My dad used to chant a song most of his life, "I was born in Mississippi but I'm gonna die in Tennessee." He traveled the world with the Air Force and spent most of his life living overseas. He was living in England toward the end of his life when out of the blue, he got transferred to the States. Guess which state he ended up in? You guessed it—Tennessee. He confessed what ended up being a self-fulfilling prophecy. You will eat the fruit of your words. What are you saying? Watch your mouth!

I had to change my language and my patterns and how I spoke about certain things. Whenever I saw a deficiency in my life—things about myself that were not as they should be, either in the moment or when I was journaling and doing self-reflection—God would give me confessions to say. I had to confess these daily to shift my thinking, my mind, and the way I saw everything in my environment.

Even Mike had to learn that. I would remind him, "There's power in your tongue. There's power in your tongue." One time he was having a conversation with the boys, lecturing them about something, and said something negative. I went to praying and casting down what he'd said. One of the kids looked over and asked, "What is Mama doing?" Mike said, "Don't pay any attention to your mama. She's over there casting down what I said." He knew.

A book called *The Creative Power of God,* by Charles Capps, taught me the power of confession. He called these little confessions he got from the Word of God *God's pills.* He wrote that if I said these confessions every day, then I would see the thing I was confessing happen.

We had a house in Bentonville we had moved out of and were trying to sell. One day a storm had caused water to get in through a broken piece of flashing, and the wet wood started to grow mold in the house. Whenever you say "mold," people lose interest. This was a brand-new house we had built, but once people who were interested in buying the house heard the word "mold," they would run away. *The Creative Power of God* had a section in it with confessions about selling a house. I started commanding my house to sell. We had had the house for over a year, but I started saying those confessions every day and every time I would think about the house, and in two weeks the house sold. I knew it was God because the buyer, when we told him the house had mold, said, "I don't care about that; just give me the paperwork, and I'll sign it." That's one instance where my confessions have shifted my life.

MASTERING SHAME

I have been embarrassed about my behavior sometimes, especially my inability to cope with some situations. Mike told me, "You've got to learn how to communicate with people because we're going to frequently be around people you don't know." I was not comfortable talking to people I didn't know. He helped me to become more outgoing, to even talk to random people. He pulled me out of my shell and got me going.

Because we were moving every two years—we wound up moving eleven times (so far) in our marriage—every two years I had to learn how to make new friends and create another new community for myself. Moving around pulled out another aspect of me I never knew was possible. I thought it was the worst thing that could happen to me, but it was one of the best things.

POSITIVE COMMUNICATION

In my marriage, I had to learn positive, constructive communication. I had to learn who my husband is because when you're in a marriage, you have two different personalities trying to work together. You have to pick your battles. You need to know when to lean back and back out, when to push and when to pull. There's always an exchange going on. You've got to know what your boundaries are. I knew it was wrong to talk to him in a derogatory way. When you're in a marriage, you should not degrade your husband or communicate with him in a way that demeans his character or who he is.

Anytime you say something abrasive to your husband, he holds back that thought process he was about to share. He never forgets it, even if you are playing. I had to learn to master my tone and temperament, and my greatest lesson started with my husband.

I knew early on I needed to change the narrative in my marriage because in my large family we are fighters. Either you speak up boldly or you get run over. I couldn't do that with Mike. I had to learn how to not suppress but learn the dynamics of give and take in marriage.

When you're in an argument with any person, you may think, *I'm not going to lose this argument*. You want to get your point across. The goal is to impress your opinion on the other person, but when you're in a marriage, that's not productive. You may win the argument, but it's a loss overall because you have left your husband broken down; you lose even in winning. It's not the thing to do. I had to learn a better way to communicate in my marriage or there was no way we would have been able to stand the test of time. In my workplace I was outspoken too, and that never worked out for me.

One of the keys to provoking positive change in your life is to identify patterns and cycles in different arenas—be they in your family, your professional life, your relationships, and even in your friendships. If you pay attention, God will speak about your patterns through your circumstances. He showed me my cycles in my workplace, and I came to terms with the fact I was a bully. A friend of mine informed me that people were afraid to talk to me. I had never realized it before. I thought I was setting good boundaries and making it clear to people what I expected of them. *Here I am. I'm in my own space. If I don't speak to you or say anything to you, leave me alone.* My friend said, "No, you're creating a hostile environment that makes you unapproachable. People feel they can't talk to you because you lash out verbally." I began to deal with me. *I* was the problem. That's not what I'm trying to portray. I don't want to be *that* person.

MASTERING FAITH

I got married at nineteen. I didn't have kids until I was twenty-six, not because I wanted to wait but because we were having problems getting pregnant. I had never used any kind of contraception, but I was not able to have a baby, and I didn't understand why. Once I realized we had been trying that long and had not conceived, I thought something was wrong with me. We went to a fertility doctor to see if there were any problems. I had fibroids, but other than that, I should have been able to get pregnant. The doctor put me on a fertility medication, which I started taking in faith that God would use it to help me conceive. It wasn't effective immediately, but I kept taking it, kept praying, and kept trying.

One day a year later, I was craving beer. I don't drink, but I went to the store and bought a six-pack of beer. My husband asked, "What is this? What are you doing?" I said, "I don't know. I'm craving beer," and he said, "You better go and check—maybe you're pregnant or something." I took a test and it came up positive. But then I said, "We better get another one to be sure, and maybe get two more." Every test kept coming up positive, and that's when we knew I was pregnant. We went to the clinic to get blood test verification, and they confirmed it. We were elated.

We heard another couple at the clinic saying, "Oh, we got twins," and they were excited about having twins. I looked at Mike and said, "Man, I wish we could have twins." Then the following week we came back for another visit, and during the ultrasound they kept bringing people in. I asked what was wrong, and the doctor said, "We said it's one, but now it's two!" A double blessing.

— 11 —

FINANCIAL BREAKTHROUGH

Prosper as your soul prospers

I experienced two schools of thought regarding finances growing up. One was to live for today and spend money like there was no tomorrow. Another way of thinking was to always save for a rainy day because rain would surely come. I saw those around me with no regard for honoring their word and not paying when they said they would pay. I saw others who were faithful to pay their bills on time, no matter what, even if they had to sacrifice their own personal needs to make do. I decided I would not be financially irresponsible, no matter what. I decided we would not live check to check, no matter what. I decided we would be financially free, no matter what. I would manage my finances the right way.

I decided I wanted to work hard for anything I earned. I never wanted to owe anybody a debt. I dislike even the perception of debt. Early on in my marriage, I noticed I had a lot of bad financial habits. I didn't grow up rich at all. I do remember, however, growing up never looking at the cost of things. We just bought whatever we wanted no matter the cost. I would gather all I wanted in the store and when the check totaled, I would be blown away at the amount, but I would never put anything back. I never really fully understood the real cost of things and the time it would take to repay whatever I charged on my credit cards. I later realized I was handling my life horribly in the finance department. I was not being a good steward over what God had given me financially. This was not God's best for us. "Beloved, I wish above all things that thou mayest prosper and be in health, even as thy soul prospereth" (3 John 1:2).

My husband was working in management in corporate America at the time. He got paid large bonus checks of $50,000 or more. We would take the money and buy new things. We'd refurnish our whole house until all the money was gone. We never saved anything. He was making six figures, and I was making close to six figures, but it was like we had holes in our pocket. We didn't have anything we kept. We saved just enough, but not to where we were seeing major multiplication in our finances.

I was the kind of person who had worked two or three jobs if I needed to pay off debt. I did that for a season—I worked two jobs back to back. I had one job I worked from 3 a.m. to 11 a.m., and then I would go right into the next job from 11 a.m. to 7 p.m. I worked eighty hours a week just to pay our debts, and then I realized this debt thing is terrible. Most of the debt came from my shopping habits by the way. My husband could hold on to a dollar for weeks. So he was definitely not the problem. It's like I had an *aha* moment. *I don't want to work like this. I don't want to live like this. I don't want to be in debt. I want to have more than enough.*

Then my perspective about finances started to shift. I started having a hunger to get more information about finances, how to make investments, which investments to choose, which types of things grew wealth for people. I studied the habits of wealthy people to see how I could integrate some of this into my life to see a valuable change in my own finances, and that's when everything about how I operated my finances shifted.

We were paying tithes sporadically until God rooted the foundational truth of the power of reaping and sowing and the power of the tithe in me. At first I believed in it alone. My husband was kind of shifty about it. He said, "I don't understand why we've got to do that." I finally got him on board, but then I started seeing the size of the tithe checks we were writing and thinking, *Wow, this is a lot of money.* My husband said to me one day, "Just write the check. You don't worry about it. God blessed us." Now it was him helping me because the enemy was trying to plant all kinds of seeds in my head about giving, especially, giving back to God. That's the great thing about being equally yoked in marriage—when one is weak, the other can be strong. If you both are weak, there is mass confusion, chaos, and debt like crazy.

My husband and I did a Dave Ramsey Financial Freedom class that really helped us begin to see the importance of not having debt even more clearly. We took tips from different financial gurus, and we created the best financial plan for our lives that was strongly rooted and based on the Word of God.

You will never conquer and overcome what you cannot recognize. Most people get so caught up in the appearance of having money that they relinquish and forfeit their peace, happiness, and freedom just feed their vanity. When you are in a cycle, you never stop to think *Why am I doing this?* You are doing it because you have always done it that way. This is why most of our nation is in financial ruin, as well as our country. We exist for a "live now and pay later—way, way later" reality. We are good as long as the bill doesn't show up right away. This is not what God intended at all for us. "For the Lord your God will bless you as he has promised, and you will lend to many nations but will borrow from none. You will rule over many nations but none will rule over you" (Deuteronomy 15:6 NIV). I totally understand there will be times when you need to borrow, but the intent should always, always be debt freedom.

Proverbs 22:7 says "The rich rule over the poor, and the borrower is slave to the lender" (NIV). Ever wonder why so many relationships are destroyed over money? This is why Mike and I have made a rule to not lend money to family or friends. It has been our experience that family is the worst; they put you last on the list to get repaid. They think you should always understand their situation. Yes, they always have some sort of situation going on as to why they cannot repay what they promised you they would pay back. Their income tax refund shows up and they're driving new cars and there's still no check for you. Family can be the most inconsiderate of them all. Friends are not that far behind. This is why no matter what, I refuse to lend to family and friends. If you want your close relationships with your family and friends to remain intact, never, ever lend money. If what you are reading upsets you in any way, then you may be the family or friend I'm referring to. It's time to grow up and mature in ensuring your financial future is strong.

People often get it confused. Most think that the more money you make, the better. This is a total falsity. Have you ever noticed how lottery winners lose millions and wind up broke? It's because their mind-set about money didn't change. You will always lose any money that comes in with the wrong mind-set. You will never ever have enough. One thing I know for sure I that it's not about how much you make, it's about what you do with what you keep. Even more importantly, learning about money and understanding how to make it work for you, instead of you working for it, is a total game changer.

MASTERING ENTREPRENEURSHIP

Early on, God planted a seed inside our hearts. He told us we were entrepreneurs. We knew we were; we just didn't know how to get there. There was much trial and error on our part. For instance, my husband loved golf. One day he decided he was going to open a golf store. Who opens a golf store? Who shops there? So he had a guy come out, he talked to the guy, and we went and looked at buildings. What I didn't know is that just to get the man to negotiate and to initiate this process, Mike had to pay a down payment of $17,000. Here I was thinking we were just brainstorming the idea, not knowing he was full-out invested. I felt deep down inside that this was not what God intended for us, but I didn't know how to get my husband to know this was not what he was called to do. I knew it would diminish everything inside him. I saw a golf store really stifling his growth. I felt like he was much bigger than that; not that it was a totally bad idea, but I knew a golf store as the only business venture was not enough for what I felt was inside him.

He has such a brilliant business mind, and I knew this store was going to hamper everything. I said, "No, this is not what you're supposed to do. This is not it." Later we wound up losing the $17,000—the cost to learn a valuable lesson. We had to chalk it up to life's tuition. But what seemed like a failure really was an opportunity to pivot. The greatest lesson we learned in that experience was to not give up. Our hearts were set; we were entrepreneurs no matter what happened.

Mike had always worked in corporate America. He worked in leadership positions with a Fortune 500 company for twenty years, and after that he wound up taking a job at Pizza Hut as an area coach, where he ran five to seven stores for five years. He climbed the ranks in a five-year span from an area coach job into high-level roles into then being over all the corporately-owned Pizza

Hut equity stores, which were about 500 stores or so.

I asked him if we could buy those stores if they ever sold them. I wanted him to ask, but he said no, we could never afford that. "Do you know how much these stores cost?" I said, "No, we couldn't afford it, but God could. Yeah, that's a multimillion-dollar package, but if God wants us to have it, then ... you know?" And he just looked at me like I was crazy. I was thinking, *Okay, I'm talking to the wind.* But God gave me a plan. The spirit of God was being strategic and leading us through this process. He told me how to pray. My prayer life began to totally shift. I would pray before, but I would always pray by myself until God gave me the instruction to begin praying with my husband. Once Mike heard me pray, he told me, "You just keep on praying because I like what you're doing. Something special is going on with you with this prayer thing." He said, "You pray, you pray."

We prayed together every day about our business and for God to give us guidance. The Holy Spirit told me how to strategically pray for favor, specifically that we would have favor with corporate and with the banks. And we did. Then God told me, "Now you need to pray for divine connections." I prayed for the connections. I prayed God would start bringing the right people in so my husband would be able to discern how to assemble our team.

Mike had trained everybody in this area because he worked his way up and he put the right people and leaders in place. I couldn't have planned this better myself. It was such a God thing that he would create his leadership team and his business model while in the employment of the corporation that would later just pass the baton over to him with everything already in position. He didn't have to make any changes; he just added a few key leadership positions and a human resources team. God sent us all the right people to connect with. The creation of our business was a total God thing because there is no way we could have done any of this on our own. Absolutely no way! God gets all the glory for everything that transpired in our business. Every single detail was a part of God's divine plan.

MASTERING SAVING

When I was working as an RN, God told me to invest half of my check into a certain investment. I thought it was bizarre because when I would get my check, I'd be so frustrated. *Why am I not paying myself? Why am I sending half of my money to this investment fund?* But the thing about it was that God even told me which fund to put the money into. This fund was multiplying my investment exponentially. It was rolling over my money so quickly that even the investment people of the fund would call me and say, "Who told you to do this? This is way too aggressive. At your age you should not be investing so aggressively. You should be more moderate, you know? And who told you to put all your money in this fund?"

It was the Holy Ghost who told me because He knew this deal was coming. It was my retirement, and if I hadn't listened to Him back then, I wouldn't have accrued the amount of money I needed to start this new business. I put all of my retirement fund into this new business venture and earned the majority of the money we needed completely on the leading of the Holy Spirit. If I hadn't listened, this would have never come to pass; we would have missed the opportunity completely. Mike had the stocks and the retirement amount we needed, but because he was employed there, *they wouldn't release it to him.* We had some other investments, but for various reasons, they were all tied up and could not be liquidated at the time. God worked everything out perfectly. Whenever I take a moment to look back over everything that transpired, I realize more than ever that God's hand was over every aspect of the deal.

I wrote a prayer in my journal during the time when everything in the natural was saying it would never happen for us and that we didn't have enough money to afford it.

> Help me, Lord God, with all the things I need help with. Do *not* let me miss this opportunity to be an entrepreneur. Show me what I should do.
>
> Give me and Mike favor with you and with men. Send down negotiation strategies and download heaps on heaps of wisdom unto us. Send us helpers to assist and support us—heavenly angels to begin to minister to me. Dispatch your heavenly angels to help us to bring this deal to fruition. I command, decree, and declare a great release of provision, resources, wealth transfers, mind shifts, realignment, promotion, and increase in all areas of our lives. In Jesus's name, amen.

God had often told me my husband and I were called to be entrepreneurs, and not just that, but we were also called to function in a high level of business and wealth. God had given us both a desire to become entrepreneurs. God even began to send prophets and other prophetic voices to confirm everything He had planted in our hearts. Now it was time to walk it all out in faith.

Most people treat me differently when they realize we own multiple franchises. Some responses are positive but a lot are negative. As a result, I would oftentimes be reluctant to share my testimony with most people. However, the Word of God says we overcome the enemy by the word of our testimony. I never want to give off the air that I've made it or that I am all that, nor do I want people to come to me only for money or connections, but I must share my testimony.

When someone asks what my husband does for a living, I say, as a black woman, "My husband works for Pizza Hut." Most people automatically think because he's black that he's in there cutting up and boxing pizzas. Most people would never imagine that we could be owners. God dealt with my heart about that. He said, "Do you think I blessed you with that and shifted your life in that direction to keep it to yourself? No. I did it for you because you have to share the story of how I transferred the wealth into your hands." He shifted our lives completely. Owning those franchises was nothing we could have done in our own strength. But with God *all* things are possible.

The Holy Spirit said, "People are going to start coming to you for things, so your discernment level needs to come up. I'll begin to show you who's for you and who is against you, and you'll know where *to* invest, where *not* to invest, who to link up with, who to connect with, and who to make alliances with." He told me, "I'll tell you all of this, and you don't have to worry about it." I would often think to myself, *I just don't want to be deceived. I don't want people to use me.* It's a horrible feeling when people come into your life for the wrong reasons or try to take advantage of you. That's a pet peeve of mine. I was always the one in school who took up for the person who was getting taken advantage of. To this day, if people don't have a voice, I will have a voice for them.

— 12 —

MASTERING YOU

Conclusion

SINCE MASTERY IS A CONSTANT STATE of evolution, I believe I have matured more in my own skin. I've started to overcome some fears of mine that had escalated in my mind as mountains. I do this by stepping out and doing the things God has called me to do. This helps in stretching and enlarging my capacity to be exactly who God created me to be.

I gave my life group an assignment a few months ago, and I want to offer it to you as well.

FIND YOUR STRENGTHS

1. List 2–3 major fears you have avoided in your life. Try to include the fear people ask you about the most. For example, I was extremely fearful of public speaking, but people are always asking me to speak at their events. These are what I call God-directional moments. God is pointing you toward the thing you were destined to do, but the enemy is encasing it with fear to create a total avoidance of the very thing God has called you to do.

2. Ask at least 3–5 people (the more the better) to list at least 3–5 of your strengths or one thing you are really good at.

What we found was we avoided the very things others viewed as our strengths. I had accepted leadership roles in the workplace but had outright refused leadership roles in other areas in my life because I felt uncomfortable in them. The interesting thing was that others listed my strengths as being a leader, forward thinker, visionary leader, and wealth strategist. They said I am bold, confident, knowledgeable, courageous, resourceful, smart, trustworthy, and more. My fear was lying to me.

The story we tell ourselves is an alternate reality of the truth. Our alternate realities are plagued with self-limiting beliefs as a result of our childhood, word curses that have been spoken over us by broken people and past experiences. All these things tend to formulate our thought process.

Until your soul is healed in this area, you will always be fostering an alternate reality and allowing it to thrive in your mind. This is especially the truth for those who think everyone is out to get them or that it's always someone else's fault for why their life is not progressing. It's time you take ownership for your life and your current circumstances and do the work. It's needed and it's necessary.

Achieving mastery in life is an overall spiritual journey. The more you learn about yourself, the more adjustments you can make for your spiritual growth. Hosea 4:6 says "my people are destroyed from a lack of knowledge." God has given us a command to grow in knowledge or die, perish, and cease to exist. It's important we continue to expand our knowledge base in all areas of our lives.

If your finances are a place of contention for you, then study finances. Learn and study what God has to say about money and finances first, then all the other books are just supplemental. The Word of God is always the foundation on which we need to build all our knowledge upon.

We allow things to exist in our lives because we've always seen things done that way by our family and friends and the way they deal with circumstances. You allow certain things to exist because you don't know God has already dealt with them and that any struggle or toil in your life is a manifestation of the curse. Any resemblance of toil, lack, poverty, sickness, or disease is a direct contradiction to what God has given you in His Word. Learn His promises. He's already promised to make you to prosper. You don't have to wonder what your next step will be; you need to just start with God. As long as you seek Him, He's going to give you the supernatural ability to obtain these things. Focus on the promises of God, and make the appropriate adjustments in your life to comply with heaven's mandate.

- What promises are in the Word of God that I can now confess daily to reap God's best for my life?

- What mind-sets or thought processes have limited my growth spiritually, mentally, physically, and financially?

- What things am I willing to change about myself to receive God's best?

- What relationships do I continue to foster, even though I know they are negative and unhealthy for my life?

- How do I plan to build healthy relationships going forward?

- What is one action I can complete today toward something God has instructed me to do? What's the next action I can complete? And so on. Deuteronomy 28:12 NKJV says God will bless the works of your hands, but how can He if you are not doing anything?

- Find a mentor or a coach—someone who
  o pours into you,

- o teaches you how to be the best version of yourself,
- o hears from God,
- o walks with God,
- o will build you up and never tear you
  down,
- o will encourage and empower you,
- o is not fearful or jealous of your
  strengths because she knows exactly who she is,
- o is doing the thing you feel you were
  called to at the level you want to do
  it in.

Now take notes and shift. You are well on your way!

It is very dangerous to be out of alignment with God. There is protection when you are in alignment with God. So many great benefits are extended in the place of godly alignment. "But the Lord is faithful, and he will strengthen you and protect you from the evil one" (2 Thessalonians 3:3 NIV). "Though I walk in the midst of trouble, you preserve my life. You stretch out your hand against the anger of my foes; with your right hand you save me" (Psalm 138:7 NIV). To achieve the fullness of your God-ordained destiny, you have to be in alignment with God.

It's important we stay in alignment with God's plans and purposes and not our own. When we hold fast to our own agendas, we lose out on destiny fulfillment. When Elijah decided he was tired and didn't want to continue on anymore, God raised up Elisha to take his place. Don't let that be you! You don't want to wake up one day seeing someone else doing the thing God called you to do, knowing that because of your stubbornness or paralyzing fear, you failed to see it come to pass. There is no need to get upset or mad with someone else for being brave enough to seize the moment.

There are levels and dimensions in God. No one will ever know everything there is to know about God and this spiritual experience we are having on earth. All I know is that the more I know and understand about God, the more I grow in relationship with Him, the more I want to please Him and do what He has called me to do on earth.

It is imperative that we all position our hearts to be lifetime students striving for more and more of God's wisdom. Our natural knowledge is okay, but the wisdom of God is what I'm after. If nations can be shifted into positions of power and influence by the Word of God, then I, too, can shift into my perfect position in the kingdom, and so can you.

NOTE FROM TONYA

This book was truly a labor of love. I wanted to share how my past experiences either strengthened me or flawed my thought process. Even my subsequent actions and how I viewed the world around me were the results of a defective processing system in my mind. I struggled with identity issues, insecurity, rejection, shame, condemnation, bitterness, anger, and low self-esteem. God had to shift my entire perspective by daily renewing my mind with the Word of God.

Oftentimes, we need help seeing things through the eyes of Christ. It was not until I began to develop a relationship with God that my entire life began to shift for the better. This book is meant to give you real-life accounts of situations and circumstances that began to mold my thinking, my actions, and even my reactions to those around me.

I pray this book will be the beginning of an awakening for you, and that you will begin to seek God for all He has for your life. My recommendation is that you do the work—the hard, difficult, and frustrating work to becoming the best version of yourself possible. God has placed so much potential in you. It's time you begin to shift your mind-set into a world beyond what you can see— one that can only be revealed through relationship with God.

Tonya Howard Quinn

ABOUT THE AUTHOR

Tonya Howard Quinn is just a girl who loves Jesus. She is passionate about sharing the God of relationship with whomever she meets.

A prophetic voice called to empower women, Tonya is a visionary leader and a wealth strategist. She is also an author, speaker, mentor, and coach. She teaches and advises women how to transition into entrepreneurship and create businesses. She leads a women's life group at her church called Mastering Me, in which she teaches, trains, and develops women into living their God-ordained destiny.

She is called to dominate in the sphere of business. She and her husband currently own sixty-three restaurant franchises throughout Mississippi, Louisiana, and Florida. She and her husband continue to grow and prosper their business by following God's instruction.

Tonya is a family nurse practitioner by profession. She is passionate about creating opportunities to close the healthcare gap by providing more available and affordable access to patient care throughout Mississippi.

FOLLOW TONYA

www.tonyahowardquinn.com

ACKNOWLEDGMENTS

To my husband: You have been the wind beneath my wings. You have always pushed me to greater heights. You are always asking me the tough questions that cause me to shift into deeper and greater dimensions of who God has called me to be. Thanks for reflecting back to me the truth of what needs to be dealt with, adjusted, commended, and celebrated.

To my sons: I love you to the moon and back. Thank you for being God's instruction tool in my life. I am constantly learning from our conversations and interactions. The best things in life are truly our children. I love you guys!

To my mom: You have been a story of great strength and tenacity, beating all the odds that told you to fail. You have risen above and beyond every circumstance that was meant to defeat and destroy you. It's time you realize that fully. And for that I would like to say *bravo!*

To my Mastering Me life group: You all have shown me what real girl power is all about. You have shown me what true sisterhood looks like. You are the group God built with His own majestic hands. Thanks for holding me accountable and for never allowing me to forget what I was called to do, to build, and to create in the earth. Love you guys!

CAN YOU HELP?

REVIEWS ARE EVERYTHING TO AN AUTHOR BECAUSE
THEY MEAN A BOOK IS GIVEN MORE VISIBILITY. IF YOU
ENJOYED THIS BOOK, PLEASE REVIEW IT ON YOUR
FAVORITE BOOK REVIEW SITES AND TELL YOUR FRIENDS
ABOUT IT. THANK YOU!

www.ingramcontent.com/pod-product-compliance
Lightning Source LLC
Chambersburg PA
CBHW072149090426
42740CB00012B/2192